CHANGE
IS THE RULE

Practical Actions for Change: On Target, On Time, On Budget

Winford E. "Dutch" Holland, Ph.D.

Executive Editor, Holland & Davis, Inc. Change Library

DEARBORN™
A **Kaplan Professional** Company

This publication is designed to provide accurate and authoritative information in regard to the subject matter covered. It is sold with the understanding that the publisher is not engaged in rendering legal, accounting, or other professional service. If legal advice or other expert assistance is required, the services of a competent professional should be sought.

Acquisitions Editor: Jean Iversen
Managing Editor: Jack Kiburz
Project Editor: Trey Thoelcke
Interior Design: Lucy Jenkins
Cover Design: Design Alliance, Inc.
Typesetting: Elizabeth Pitts

Published by Dearborn
A Kaplan Professional Company

Special permission to use Capability Maturity Model® for Software (Version 1.1) CMU/SEI-93-TR-024, ©1993 by Carnegie Mellon University is granted by the Software Engineering Institute.

CMM® and Capability Maturity Model® are registered in the U.S. Patent and Trademark Office.

Printed in the United States of America

00 01 02 10 9 8 7 6 5 4 3 2 1

Library of Congress Cataloging-in-Publication Data

Holland, Winford E.
    Change is the rule : practical actions for change, on target, on time,
on budget / Winford E. "Dutch" Holland.
    p. cm.
Includes bibliographical references and index.
ISBN 0-7931-3612-1 (hb)
1. Organizational change. 2. Leadership. Management. I. Title.
HD58.8.H65 2000
658.4'063—dc21   99-086729

PRAISE FOR *CHANGE IS THE RULE*

"What a great uncluttered roadmap for understanding, embracing, and leading change. We have trained over 10 million leaders worldwide, and change is their biggest challenge. This book should be next on their reading list!"

> Dr. Paul Hersey
> Chairman, Center for Leadership Studies

"*Change Is the Rule* will be among the required reading for my executive leadership team as we continue to drive for dramatic business growth and value creation for Texaco in the highly competitive domestic energy markets."

> W. Robert Parkey, Jr.
> President, Texaco Natural Gas Inc.

"Dutch Holland provides the clearest, most practical guidance imaginable on integrating the running of any business with implementing changes necessary to assure future success."

> Burt Branstetter
> Vice President and General Counsel,
> Chevron U.S.A. Production Company

"Dutch first introduced his simple winning concept 'Run-the-business/ Change-the-business' to our organization more than seven years ago. Managers who understand how to organize and handle these roles have been the key to the successful transformation of our company."

> David G. Birney
> President, Solvay Polymers, Inc.

"Change is definitely the rule in today's health-care industry. The old paradigms just don't work today, nor will they in the future. Dutch Holland offers some insightful thinking on how to manage change to create the new paradigms that all successful organizations will need in the 21st century."

> Mark A. Wallace
> President and CEO, Texas Children's Hospital

"Organization change—on target, on time and on budget—what a concept! The basics aren't new, but they're organized in a way that you want to slap yourself on the forehead and say 'why didn't I think of that!'"

> Katherine M. Tamer
> Vice President and Chief Information Officer,
> United Space Alliance

"This excellent book provides an incredibly practical guide to the critical, necessary process of change. It has significant, tangible value for all organization managers and leaders."

> Drew Alexander
> President, Weingarten Realty Investors

"Dutch Holland has compiled an easily read book on the important topic of change management. He effectively uses a simple theater analogy to illustrate and explain his key points."

> Milton D. ("Mickey") Rosenau, Jr., CMC, FIMC, NPDP
> Author of *Successful Project Management*
> and *Successful Product Development*

"Dr. Holland has identified a basic universal management theme (change) and illuminated the path toward practical ways to lead toward and implement change."

> Bette Ann Stead
> Professor, College of Business Administration/
> University of Houston

"Dutch is the most down to earth change advocate I have met in my 35 years of struggling with change. Where else do you have a University of Texas, Ph.D. that will hit you about the head to get your attention? This is not academia, this is the real world!"

> Fred Hubbard
> Sr. Vice President, Bell Helicopter Textron

"Dutch Holland's book is great reading for both experienced and relatively new executives. His use of the theater metaphor simplifies his concepts and is entertaining."

> Frank F. Ledford, Jr. M.D.
> Lt. General, USA, Retired President,
> Southwest Foundation for Biomedical Research

"A unique view of the change process containing action-oriented insights that escape many professional change agents and managers alike."

> J. Timothy McMahon
> Professor of Management, University of Houston

"The methods described in (Holland's) book and used by his firm *work* because they embrace, from first hand experience, the intricacies of how people effectively work with change and are boldly led through change."

> Alan B. Markert
> Vice President Finance, H.E. Butt Grocery Co.

"Practical, nuts-and-bolts type people, if they want to read only one book, should read this one to prepare for their next big organizational change."

> John A. D'Angelo
> Manager, Business Transformation Services,
> Schlumberger—GeoQuest

"This book is a must read for anyone trying to manage the change process. In a real life application, Marathon Ashland Petroleum LLC followed this process in forming a successful merger of two petroleum companies."

> J. Louis Frank
> President, Marathon Ashland Petroleum LLC

"Multiple rapid changes, successfully executed, will be the key to the 21st century business. This is a book that must be on the desk of a successful 21st century CEO."

> Major General John S. Parker, M.D.
> Commanding General, USA Medical Research
> and Material Command, Fort Detrick, MD

"This book is filled with practical guidelines and is a must read for leaders guiding their organizations through turbulent times."

> Walt Natemeyer, Ph.D.
> President, North American Training and Development

DEDICATION

To the kids in my life:
the big kids, Eric and Wendy, and the little kids, Hope and Win.

To my wife Jan for continuing support and
encouragement through thick and thin.

Thanks to my book team:
Linda Wilson, Tara Telage, Bridgett Reed, Doris Michaels,
Gerald Sindell, Jean Iversen, and Trey Thoelcke.

Way to go, Team!

Contents

Introduction

A REAL-LIFE DRAMA

The Cast

Webb: the graying and gracious CEO with change on his mind

Ann: the straight-as-a-stick, no-nonsense Senior Vice President of Operations

Toni: the "just give me the facts" CFO with the personality of a brick

Lawson: a long-time middle manager from the Sales Department

Pat: another tenured middle manager from Operations

Marty: a newly minted, but not so young, R & D manager

The action takes place in a $2 billion industrial firm struggling to stay competitive in its marketplace.

Act One, Scene One

In the company's packed, theater-style training room near the executive floor Lawson, Pat, and Marty have just taken their seats on the sixth row.

Lawson: You know what this is gonna be about, don't you? They're gonna dump another new change project into the mess we're already in.

Marty: Yeah, they probably are—but what choice do we have? Our sales are taking some real hits, and we've gotta do something.

Pat: My problem is not with the need to change . . . it's with the way we're doing it; or I should say, not doing it. We haven't even gotten through the last change. Have you guys figured out that last one?

Lawson: Well, we finally figured out what we were supposed to be doing, but we've gotten zero of the new systems we need.

Pat: Figured it out? We haven't even had time to think about it. We're absolutely covered up with work trying to deal with the customer issues being handed to us by the sales department!

Lawson: Well thanks a lot! Maybe if some of our products were made a little better, we wouldn't have customers all over us to get things right!

Marty: Come on, give it a rest. Let's hear what they have to say.

The audience quiets as the senior executives, Webb, Ann, and Toni take the stage. Webb approaches the podium and adjusts the microphone.

Webb: Ladies and gentlemen, thanks for coming to this important meeting. My goal today is to describe to you the results of the strategic planning process that the executive team has just finished. Our sales results over the last four months are no secret—and it's clear that we need to take some strong actions to get back in the game.

As I have told you before, my personal vision is for us to be number one in our industry segment. This company has a long and distinguished history of . . .

Lawson, Pat, and Marty slump down in their seats and carry on a whispered, side conversation while the three executives continue their presentations.

Lawson [out of the side of his mouth]: Didn't I tell you! More crap to put up with. And I can't believe I'm hearing the "number one" bull*#@/* again! Geez! Of course we want to be number one. Who doesn't want to be number one? I'm just waiting for someone to tell me how we are gonna do it!

Pat [in whispered reply]: Look at Toni. Chomping at the bit to give us the "gotta change and gotta do it right this time" speech. If I hear one more crack about changing on time and on budget, I'm gonna throw up!

Marty: Look at Ann. You know damn good and well that she's gonna give us the same old rah rah blah blah. "You people heard what the boss said. We're gonna buckle down and make these needed changes if we have to work seven days a week!" That old "*#@/*" hasn't given us any real guidance on the last three changes the CEO has talked about.

Lawson: Do they really expect me to go back to my troops and repeat all this garbage? I've got guys that are saving up fruit to throw at the next manager that gets up to talk about change! I'm tired of being the guy that has to take all the crap that comes out of these things.

Pat: You're singing my song, buddy. I just want to get out of here and get back to the real world!

THE RESPONSE TO
A REAL-LIFE DRAMA

Seen this play before? Or better yet, feel like you have been a part of this organizational change play? Well, the odds are that you have seen, heard about, or been a part of a real-life drama like the one you have just read. Maybe you identified with one of the three middle managers, aware of the need to change but caught up in their overwhelming workload. Maybe you identified with one of the senior executives, anxious for change but not clear on the leadership message to provide to the organization to produce successful change. Whatever your identification, the odds are that you have heard or felt some of the emotions that we just found in our characters: confusion, anxiety, frustration, weariness, cynicism, and even anger. Why? Because we are not doing organizational change right. We have not mastered change!

I label the 1980s the decade of *Change Discovery,* when companies began to see more changes in a year than they had seen in the previous decade. I label the 1990s the decade of *Change Management,* when organizations discovered that they needed to manage, not muddle through, what began to look like a continuous series of changes. I label the 2000s the decade of *Change Mastery,* when organizations finally accept the fact that change is no longer the exception but the rule. I see my clients now accepting the reality of a continuous stream of market, customer, technology, and people forces that present both problems and opportunities for future prosperity. I see companies realizing that they need to master change, to handle change really well and skillfully, both as an organization and individually.

This book is all about doing organizational change right—and doing it at a mastery level. This book is not about concepts and theories; it's about the real-world practical actions that must be taken to make organizational change work really well. Where do these practical actions come from? They come from the real world of successful change; they come from those organizations that have mastered change and have demonstrated time and again that they can make change happen—on target, on time, and on budget!

This journey to master change will not be guided by any kind of complex theory or esoteric concept. You will take your guidance primarily from a simple metaphor that most adults have already mastered. Managers and employees alike value analogies and metaphors far more than theories or concepts. I have found one metaphor that stands out as a tool for communicating and understanding organizations and organizational change. What is that metaphor? The theater. I have used the theater metaphor for years to teach organizational change and found it to be virtually universally understood by managers.

> An organization can be thought of as a theater company that gives a satisfying performance to an audience of customers. Before discounting this metaphor as outlandish, consider that most of you get up each morning, put on your work clothes (costume), travel to your company (the theater), walk into your office (the set), and execute your job (role) according to the organization's goals and objectives (the script) to deliver products and/or services to customers (the audience)—until it's time to go home to start all over again the next day.
>
> In the theater metaphor, organizational change would be the equivalent of a theater company moving from an existing play to a new one, requiring the transition of company roles, costumes, and sets. Imagine that a theater company, with a dwindling audience for its current performance of *Romeo and Juliet,* decides to make the move to a fresh version of *My Fair Lady.* In the theater, change mastery is critical because no play lasts forever: change is the rule.

So let's get on with the drama of organizational change. Let's be guided by the simple metaphor of the theatrical performance. Let's master change as many companies have already mastered it. But first, let me describe my experience with this fascinating subject of change.

MY EXPERIENCE WITH ORGANIZATIONAL CHANGE

My organization, Holland & Davis, (the *we* in this book) and I have had to learn change over the past three decades. Engagement after engagement has involved some form of change: companies wanting assistance in changing direction, structure, processes, assets, or people performance. As consultants we are never hired to help a company serve its customers, but to help the organization change the way it is serving customers and generating revenue.

Sometimes I find myself wondering how and why I got so deeply involved in the change game. Our firm obviously likes to work in change—we have learned a lot and been well rewarded over the last few decades. But perhaps my interest in change came from my first steps in the real-world work environment.

Without realizing it at the time, I had some great opportunities to learn change through two early experiences in special organizations: the U.S. Air Force and NASA. Both of these organizations knew a great deal about successfully managing change and lived in environments where change was the rule. They had change processes in place, and they pulled off big, complex, important changes on a regular basis with infrequent failures. At the heart of their approaches to change was what I now call the most important right idea about change: *change is primarily a mechanical process with social implications that can be systematically managed without being chaotic or out of control.*

During my time as a very young pilot in the United States Air Force, I saw and was a part of the well-planned change approach that was used to continuously upgrade the mission capability of the Strategic Air Command (SAC). For SAC, change was clearly the rule and not the exception as it sought to keep its capabilities at the leading edge. Decommissioning an outmoded weapons system while commissioning a new state-of-the-art one is a major change in anybody's book, involving billions of dollars in hard assets, and tens of thousands of people in locations dispersed all over the world. SAC made this kind of big-league change on a frequent basis—without a hitch and with personnel actually feeling challenged, involved, and, dare I say it, having fun despite the incredibly high stress on themselves and their families. I vividly remember flying the current aircraft by day and studying by night to be able to fly the newest aircraft—although in SAC that schedule was frequently reversed! The continuous, systematic approach to change that I lived with each and every day clearly had a long-term positive effect on both my attitudes and skills for change.

I was fortunate also to spend six years working inside NASA's Manned Spacecraft Center (now the Johnson Space Center) from 1970 to 1976, when change was the rule. It was a time that saw the culmination of the Apollo missions to the moon; the first U.S.-Russian space project, the Apollo-Soyuz Test Project; the first space station, Skylab; and the beginning of the Space Shuttle era. My job was to work with the young Turks who were to become NASA's leaders for the eighties, nineties, and the new millennium to develop their skills around change. I was an outsider paid to be on the inside of one of the organizations that did the world class job of reliably managing complex change. While I had been exposed to both project and program management in the Air Force, my time at NASA helped me really appreciate these two management disciplines and the roles they played in systematic organizational change. I saw those disciplines being indispensable to NASA as they flew one program while developing several others in what seemed like a never-ending series of developments in space technology and capability. During this era, NASA was a true master of change—on target, on time, and on budget.

As a consulting firm, we have also been fortunate to see, up close and personal, change situations that came out of organizational tragedies. We had the opportunity to work inside Union Carbide after the Bhopal tragedy in India, inside Texaco after the declared bankruptcy resulting from the Pennzoil lawsuit, and inside NASA, for a five-year engagement after the Challenger disaster. In each of these three cases we worked with organizations that were deeply wounded by catastrophes, requiring them to do much soul searching about recovery and future possibilities. We have seen managers and employees at the depths of work depression eventually rebound to take control of their situations and go on with the changes that needed to be made to prevent, as best as possible, future recurrence. In all three cases, strong leadership emerged within the organizations to focus on recovery and rebuilding. By the way, I hasten to point out to those unfamiliar with our firm that our arrival in these three organizations was *after* their tragedies—not before!

Our firm's experience has continued to grow as we have worked with up to 25 different clients per year for the last ten years. Many of these clients were dealing with major changes in their competitive environments, requiring them to change in a substantial way to avoid severe consequences. Many others were grappling with the latest management movements (some say fads)—struggling to understand the value of total quality management, reengineering, value creation, core competencies, outsourcing, strategic alliances, and virtual organizations. We noticed that in each case the client eventually came to the point of implementing something new, hopefully toward the improvement of bottom line results. We saw common patterns in the kind of organizational change and change management that were needed to bring new ideas into play.

With each of our clients we have learned new organizational change lessons and validated old ones. No two organizations have presented the exact same challenge from a consulting point of view, but patterns of right ideas and practical actions have emerged for us. Our firm has taken the role of program and/or project manager with our clients, providing them with the change management expertise and resources they need to produce results for their customers, shareholders, and employees alike.

Throughout our history we have stayed focused on the right ideas and practical actions that make successful organizational change possible. We have been fortunate to work with clients who heavily favored the practical approach to getting things done rather than the cerebral approach to understanding the theories and concepts underlying organizational change. We have been blessed with client executives who were able to appreciate our views and ask, "So what do we do, and how do we do it? We want to start right now!" We are sure that these clients have shaped our approaches as surely as we have helped shape their firms! These clients have helped us with our challenge of learning from our experiences in change management and becoming adept at translating our knowledge into practical actions based on right ideas.

ABOUT MASTERING CHANGE

This book is an attempt to connect some of the right ideas about organizational change to practical actions that can be used by any employee or manager to understand and act on change. My approach will not be to use theory to make key points; instead I will focus on detailed actions needed for organizational change.

This book will be new to many because it is based on ideas of the organization as a *mechanical system*. Also new will be the explicit consideration of organizational change while an organization is doing its day-to-day business of serving customers and making money for its stockholders. Every manager who has tried to guide an organizational change has experienced the reality of having to run the business while changing the business.

This book will continue to use the theater metaphor to describe organizations and organizational change. It will show organizations as analogous to theater companies that act out a play that satisfies customers. I will continue to use theater examples as a way of clearing the mind of organizational change clutter so that you can see how wrong some of the accepted organizational change ideas are.

This book will give you the logical tools you will need to better understand the organization you are a part of. You will see organizational change as a set of actions that must be performed for there to be change results. The theater metaphor will always be available to you as you think through an organizational change: "Let's see now, if this were a theater company, we would be asking the actors to . . . !"

You will see that the actions identified in this book are not that different from the actions you have already been performing as an employee or manager in a modern organization. You will realize that the day-to-day management tools already within your competence are the key tools needed for successfully changing organizations—if used in the change context I will explain in this book.

As a reader of this book you will master change, a subject that has not likely been a part of your business education. You will no longer feel lost during organizational change—you will have a road map for change that you can confidently follow. You will know what concrete things to do and when to do them. You will know what to expect of employees and how to handle them during the change process. You will be able to manage and communicate change that is not life or ego threatening to you or your employees. You will be able to continue to run your business while changing it.

Best of all, you will never again look at organizational change as a mysterious experience to be feared and fought. You will see organizational change as a creative act of leadership than can be done—*on target, on time, and on budget!*

PART ONE

The State of Change

Organizations are changing at a record pace to keep up with a business environment that demands more performance. Some organizations are doing a good job of changing to meet new performance requirements. These organizations know that change is the rule and that they will need to master change to continue to thrive. But not all companies have grasped the importance of becoming skilled and proficient at change. Many of these companies are still hanging on to the old idea about change: Don't worry about this latest change. It too shall pass. Worse yet, many organizations are using very ineffective approaches to organizational change; approaches that yield partial success at best and, in many cases, outright failure.

Organizations no longer need to muddle through changes. We know enough about organizations in change to be able to offer a curriculum for mastering change. Fortunately, there are approaches that work for companies that want to become more proficient at change. As more companies begin to use the knowledge in the curriculum for mastering change, the overall state of organizational change will change for the better!

1

The Need to Master Organizational Change

THE NEED FOR PROFICIENCY IN CHANGING ORGANIZATIONS

Over the years we have been fortunate to work for many good managers—managers commanding everything from multi-million dollar operations to multi-billion dollar, global enterprises. A dominant impression we formed while working with these managers is their confidence and competence in running their far-flung businesses. Despite good bottom-line results, we have frequently seen these competent and confident managers frustrated by their organizations' lack of proficiency in change. We have worked alongside them during many tough times of change and have helped them become alert to the need for good decision making in the management of change.

Fortunately, our firm and most of the executives we work with have witnessed or heard about change decisions that their makers wished they could recall. Take some of the following cases for example:

> The president of a major international industrial products company challenged his company with developing a new culture—one characterized by more open communication, participation, and employee involvement. The president delivered his message in an auditorium setting, complete with microphone and written notes (which he read)—with no questions allowed! Later on, he

3

admitted that his method of delivery wasn't exactly in sync with the open participative theme of his message!

The executive team of one of the major energy companies was frustrated with how long it was taking to get its change initiatives implemented. When asked how many change initiatives were being implemented, the team didn't know. One executive took it upon himself to inventory the initiatives that were in some way backed by the president and his executive team of seven. The inventory showed over 70 initiatives that were percolating down through the organization. Of the 70 initiatives, only a dozen or so had an assigned owner who was accountable for actual implementation. Without meaning to, management was collectively drowning its employees in change!

After completing a thorough strategic planning exercise, the top executive in a high-technology services company was positive that the new product line just completing its testing would be both the company's high margin line and the best hope for revitalizing the company's image in the marketplace. But when the senior vice president of sales came for approval of his proposed salesman incentive structure for the new line, the executive insisted that the sales commission for the new line should be exactly the same as that of the older, easier-to-sell, low margin lines! After six months of poor sales of the new line, the exec was forced to say "OOPS!"

How can these cases occur? My consultants and I at Holland & Davis have observed over the years that it is one thing to be able to use an existing organization to serve customers and make money for stockholders, and it is another thing entirely to be able to make fundamental changes in the way that the organization operates. Running a business and changing a business are two different kinds of jobs—each requiring different mindsets and skill sets. That wouldn't be a problem if changes didn't come along often and a company could just keep doing what it had been doing and still satisfy customers and stockholders. But today's business environment is very different than it was a few short years ago, and change is now the rule and not the exception.

The bottom line of this book on mastering change is relatively simple. Today's business organizations have to change rapidly, and managers and employees must be able to perform as well during the change as they perform when the organization is not changing. Performing well during change means being able to execute change as well as you execute your day-to-day business—*on target, on time, and on budget.*

Unfortunately most managers and employees have been *overtrained* to perform in a no change, day-to-day business and *undertrained* to perform during change. For infrequent changes, it might be satisfactory to muddle through, but for the frequent changes called for in today's business organizations, managers and employees alike must learn to be as proficient in change as they are in running an ongoing business. And proficiency in change will only come with the learning and mastery of a set of practical actions for organizational change.

THE WAY WE ARE CHANGING ORGANIZATIONS IS NOT WORKING

The prevailing standard in running a business today is on target, on time, and on budget. Buyers expect to get what they paid for, on time, and at the price agreed to in advance. Given those buyer expectations, companies have adjusted their ways of operating in order to make this new standard a reality.

Unfortunately, there is a totally different standard in place for changing an organization: off target, very late, and way over budget. Anybody who has been a part of changing organizations has experienced changes that didn't turn out the way they were planned or that did not produce the results that were desired. They likely experienced delays of weeks, months, and even years, and cost overruns of everything from a few percentage points to orders of magnitude. Some have even experienced abandonment of organizational changes in midstream with nothing to show for it except frustration and depleted bank accounts!

A popular observation is that 70 percent of the reengineering projects that companies use to change themselves and the way they do business do not achieve the desired results. When many organization members who have gone through change look back on it and label it as nightmarish, destabilizing, chaotic, and life changing, we know that something is ineffective! It's time to question the way we go about changing organizations.

Are all companies having trouble changing? For companies who have not had to change very often, the occasional change is especially difficult but they usually muddle through. For companies more experienced with organizational change, the change process goes better.

But even the companies who do change best cannot do it as well as they can run their daily businesses. Of those companies best at change, few would be willing to adopt a change standard of on target, on time, and on budget. And therein lies the problem; companies are not changing well enough to avoid negative consequences, much less use change as a competitive weapon.

THE CASE FOR IMPROVING THE WAY WE CHANGE ORGANIZATIONS

Today's business world is dramatically different from the one we knew just a few short years ago. Greatly increased rivalry from global competitors, more demanding customers, ever-rising stockholder expectations, and accelerating technology all contribute to a business world that is different today and changing for tomorrow. Change is no longer the exception; it is now the rule!

When change was the exception, firms could win in their industries by being the best at running their day-to-day businesses—cranking out the products and services that had been winners in the market place for some time. Winning in this kind of environment was based on slowly climbing the learning curve and gradually refining work processes. Winning in this environment was very much like an automobile race run on an infinite straightaway—the winner would be the car that had the highest top speed and endurance.

Competing successfully in a world where change is the rule and not the exception requires a new standard. When change becomes the rule, firms can no longer win by being the best at running their business in an unvarying way. Now the basis for winning is how well firms can change the ways they run their businesses. The firms that win in this new business environment are those who can get new products and services into play on target, on time, and on budget. Firms that win are able to retool employee mindsets and skills on target, on time, and on budget. Firms that win are able to deploy new plants, systems, equipment, and tools, on target, on time, and on budget. Winning in this environment is very much like the automobile race run on a grand prix circuit—the winner will be the car that can get to high speed on the straights and be extremely fast through the curves.

Today's business world has raised the bar. Firms must now be able to run and change their businesses with equal proficiency. But why can't businesses already do that? Why is changing an organization so different from running one that is not changing? First, it is more difficult to change a business because you also have to keep running it! Organizations are not allowed to shut themselves down, stop serving customers, and stop paying stockholders while the company works through the change. Companies literally have to do two things at once—and that makes it difficult, time consuming, and energy depleting.

Second, companies do not know how to change with the same degree of precision with which they run their businesses. Adding to the difficulty that many companies face is what can only be charitably described as ineffective and incomplete ideas about organizational change.

EFFECTIVE AND INEFFECTIVE IDEAS ABOUT CHANGING ORGANIZATIONS

From our perspective, there are clearly some ineffective ideas about organizational change in use in the business and organizational world. We encounter ideas about what an organization is and how it functions that don't match very well with the practical reality we deal with every day as business consultants. These ineffective ideas have gradually evolved and been put into practice without very much conscious analysis or evaluation. Unfortunately, these ineffective ideas result in change methods that are bound to lead to unnecessary confusion, wasted effort, and personal hurt. These ideas carry a self-fulfilling prophecy that change is just too hard and unpredictable to be done in any kind of logical or controlled way.

We hope that by identifying these ineffective ideas we can encourage a reevaluation of some of the first properties of organizations that were identified and described many decades ago. These first-identified properties were mechanical in nature and very different than the social properties that are popular today.

The seven most common ineffective ideas about organizational change—and what we think are more effective ones—follow. I will use the theater metaphor to make it easier to see the ineffectiveness of some of today's approaches to organizational change and illustrate the right-mindedness of our more effective approach.

Ineffective Idea 1:
Organizational Change Is
Primarily a Social Process

We are not going to argue about a social process being involved. People clearly populate organizations, and they are impacted personally whenever an organization changes. Our argument is with the idea that an organization should be looked at and dealt with *mostly* like a social structure, without paying adequate attention to the other attributes of the organization. Seeing an organization as primarily a social structure has led to an overemphasis on sociological and psychological models to understand organizations and change. Organizational change is *not* akin to changing an individual personality, a marriage, a family system, or a social clique. Organizational change *is* about realigning the behaviors of people around work processes without changing who they are as individuals!

A theater director using this ineffective idea would focus her change planning almost exclusively on the social relationships enacted in the old play and how the relationships between actors would need to look in the new play—with little consideration to the requirements of the new script, not to mention the need for new costumes and sets. The director knows that the driver of new behaviors can only be the script and her mission for the play.

Effective Idea 1:
Organizational Change Is Primarily
a Mechanical Process with
Social Implications

We see organizational change as primarily a mechanical process, calling on leaders to alter the concrete attributes of organizations. The mechanical attributes of an organization—its vision, its work processes, its plant and equipment, and its contracts or agreements with its employees—must be physically altered if an organization is to change the way it does anything. Because people are involved along the way, there are social implications for the way an organization's attributes are altered. Work processes and jobs can be altered with consideration of the incumbent employees, new change direction for the alterations can be communicated clearly, and employees can be cordially invited to take part in the change—or not.

Theater directors do not treat transitioning their company to a new play as an exercise in changing the complex dynamics of social systems. Directors are focused on making the mechanical changes needed to get that new production up and running with actors in new parts, wearing new costumes on new sets.

Ineffective Idea 2:
Successful Organizational
Change Is Driven Primarily by
Excitement and Enthusiasm

This ineffective idea also stems from the view that organizational change is primarily a social process. This view holds that the excitement level of organization members is the key ingredient or driver of successful organizational change. This ineffective view causes change managers to build strong, thorough communication programs to support the desired change—and then to stop right there assuming that the major work of organizational change is done. They reason that if people know and understand what the change is supposed to do and why it is important, the change will happen successfully. Unfortunately, the result of this approach is almost always an organizational high followed by a deep organizational low as members realize that there is no gameplan of actions and resources to guide successful completion of the change.

Imagine the theater director who raises the initial excitement of cast and crew to a fever pitch with colorful images of the success of a future production and then yells "show time!" as though some magic would cause all of the transition steps between old and new performance to get done in time for opening night.

Effective Idea 2:
Organizational Excitement and
Enthusiasm Grow from Clear and
Doable Change Plans and Actions

This approach calls for change managers to work with organization members beyond the initial excitement of the vision and rationale of change to show them the detailed, coordinated action steps that will be used to make the change possible and successful. This approach produces excitement and enthusiasm in organization members as they see how they will individually and collectively fit into the change. As they begin to gain confidence that the new change will work for them, they will be willing and able to handle new tasks and responsibilities.

The competent theater director yells "show time!" only after each and every detail of the new performance has been worked through, and each and every cast member is thoroughly prepared, rehearsed, and in position for the curtain to go up.

Ineffective Idea 3:
Organizational Change Is
Art and Not Science

The idea of an organization as first and foremost a social system supports the notion that organizational change must, therefore, be art and not science. This approach has organization members convinced that they must feel their way along, experimenting as they go, as they try to change an organization to align with some new theme or concept. This approach suggests there are no orderly or logical steps that can or must be taken for effective organizational change.

A theater director using this ineffective idea would assume that he did not need a concrete gameplan to transition cast members, costumes, musical scores, and sets to meet a definite opening night schedule.

Effective Idea 3:
Changing An Organization Is
Science and Engineering,
Done with Social Finesse

Viewing an organization as a mechanical system calls for organizational change to be science and engineering more than art. This approach confirms that it is possible to derive the finite number of steps required for effective change from an analysis of the organization's present position and the statement of where the organization needs to be at some future time. These finite steps can be mapped, flow-charted and project-managed along an orderly, logical critical path—to planned schedules and budgets. The implementation of an organizational change is first and foremost a logistical problem that can be solved with careful planning and thoughtful follow through. Again, people are involved; so palatable social approaches delivered with social skills are important for change to be efficiently done with a minimum of personal disruption for managers and employees alike.

Theater directors facing the transition to a new play are well schooled in the need for precise action steps executed on time and on budget to get an acceptable performance ready for a planned opening night. And they execute those steps with the social finesse needed to get the cast and crew on board and ready.

Ineffective Idea 4:
Organizational Change Is a Social
Experiment on a Grand Scale

This ineffective idea assumes an almost infinite amount of uncertainty about any organizational change—despite any advance planning that might have been done. This approach sees organizational change as an experiment in a new social order in organizational space. The experiment may or may not work in the desired direction. This ineffective idea leaves much of the eventual results of the change to the will of the employees. If the employees like the change, it will happen. If they don't like it, it won't happen.

This ineffective idea would have a theater director launching her company toward a new performance that was both unnamed and uncertain. As the company finally settled into something it liked, the new play would be defined! Imagine selling that to theatrical investors!

Effective Idea 4:
Organizational Change Is the Planned
Modification of a Mechanical System

Changing an organization is a transition of a mechanical system from one configuration to another. The transition that must be made can be foreseen, planned, and then executed with a high degree of precision. Work processes will need to be altered or new work processes created. New or modified tools and equipment must be arranged and scheduled for installation. And employees will need to be assigned and accept new or modified roles, then trained to the needed skill level.

For the theater director there is nothing experimental about transitioning his company to a new play. The director may have some doubts about how certain actors might be able to perform in new roles, but there is no doubt about what the roles are to be. The play and roles, as well as the costumes and sets, are defined and agreed to early in the transition process.

Ineffective Idea 5:
Organizational Change Must
Occur from the Bottom Up

We know where this ineffective idea comes from; it is a misapplication of the concept of participative management that suggests that employees have good ideas too and need to be involved to be fully motivated. While there is nothing wrong with participative management, it was hardly envisioned to apply to the leadership of organization-wide change. Our complaint here is not about employees needing to buy in to change; clearly they do, and they will if it is in their interest to do so. Our argument is with the idea that somehow the proper direction for an organizational change can only come from some type of grass-roots enlightenment and initiative.

A theater director using this ineffective idea would attempt to stimulate his theater company to come up with the new play through some consensus building exercise, rather than engaging the services of a skilled playwright or choosing an existing play already proven to be a winner on Broadway!

Effective Idea 5:
Organizational Change Is a Top
Down, Leadership Exercise

Organizational change does not happen in any kind of an effective and efficient way without the presence of strong leadership providing a singular direction and coordination along the way. It is leadership that focuses the organization on its new direction, whether that direction comes first from his or her mind or from the minds of others. It is leadership that must coordinate the processes of change so that the organization does not lose its way. It is leadership that supplies the courage for continued change in the face of the inevitable resistance and disappointment along the way.

There is no doubt in the theater director's mind about the ultimate responsibility for choosing the right play. It would be hard to imagine the director explaining to investors the lack of success of a new production by suggesting that the committee of actors who chose the play must have used a flawed decision-making process.

Ineffective Idea 6:
Organizational Change Is
Inevitably Chaotic

The ineffective idea here is that organizational change is an uncoordinated social adventure with practically none of the parties involved having any real idea of what the future will hold for them or the organization. This ineffective idea sees change as a frightening misadventure that is not likely to bring as much good as it brings hurt.

A theater director using this ineffective idea would assume that the time period between an old and new performance would be totally chaotic, unplanned, unscheduled, and subject to little if any budgetary constraints!

Effective Idea 6:
Organizational Change Is Complex But
Not Chaotic Unless It Is Out of Control

Organizational change is, in most cases, complex because of the sheer number of moving parts that must be altered for the transition to be complete. But *complex* is not *chaotic*. Complexity can be managed, scheduled, and coordinated with management tools that have been around for decades. Chaos *can* enter the picture if the organization loses control of the change process by not following schedules, not doing planned things in order, or not replanning and rescheduling as actions are needed beyond the existing plan.

A theater director knows that organizational change is complex—even for a relatively small theater company—and must be planned carefully. Imagine the director explaining his company's failure to open on time by showing the transition plans he had sketched on the back of an old theater program!

Ineffective Idea 7:
Organizational Change Will
Inevitably Be Life Changing for
the Organization's Members

This ineffective idea paints organizational change as a life- and psyche-altering experience for managers and employees alike. In this approach the assumption is that managers and employees are so deeply attached to their current roles that any changes will surely be upsetting if not traumatic. While there surely are individuals who are tied to their current work at a deep psychological level, these individuals are a minority of the workforce. This approach raises the stakes for organizational change to the level that a divorce might have on family dynamics.

A theater director using this ineffective idea would certainly feel compelled to order in a team of therapists to deal with the inevitable dysfunctions that would surely arise as cast and crew found themselves traumatized after confronting the new play.

Effective Idea 7:
Organizational Change Will
Alter What People Do

Organizational change will alter what people do and how they spend their time at work, but such a change will clearly not alter who they are as individuals. Organizational change is all about getting people to alter their work behavior in ways they have altered their behaviors before, ever since they entered the workforce. Organizational change asks workers to do different things, or to do things differently—even to think about things differently—but certainly not to change their lifestyles or reasons for being. Most work changes are not so dramatic that an employee feels the desperate need to rediscover who he is to be able to continue in the employ of the company. We are not making light of the impact that a termination or layoff might have on employees, but such circumstances are the exception and not the rule in organizational change.

The director of the theater company knows she is dealing with a problem of converting an actor who is performing well in one role to performing well in another role. The director does not take on responsibility for forever changing the life of an actor because of her request that the actor plays a new role in the upcoming play.

As we move from client to client, from engagement to engagement, we see these seven ineffective ideas as part of the implicit assumptions organizations make about change. Our job with our clients is to help them see and understand the effective ideas. For us, the difference between the effective and ineffective ideas is easy to see; we have been served well by our experiences and journey in *mastering change.*

WHY TODAY'S MANAGERS DON'T HAVE A STRONG SUIT IN CHANGE

It is ironic that I need to write a book about mastering change for contemporary managers. These managers are already the ultimate change machines. From the time they start their lives, they move smoothly through development phases, changing what they do and the way they do it based on their newly developed capabilities. When they finally mature, they settle into a lifestyle fueled and excited by change —changing houses, changing cars, changing entertainment, changing foods, changing tastes in everything, thereby fueling the great consumer economy.

Nowhere in the many changes that they make on a personal basis is there much need to master change. Picking up a new car from the dealer or trying a new toothpaste is not exactly a complicated process to figure out in real time. People just get it done, and if there are a few glitches, who cares? The point of all this? We are all change animals who make changes routinely without needing training from anybody. At the personal level, we have already mastered change.

Factors that Complicate Change

Changing a business organization is a totally different matter, however. You are called on to make a much more difficult kind of change. Unlike the personal changes you might make to accommodate a new car or a new consumer product, changes in an organization have three complicating factors.

1. Organizational changes must be coordinated and integrated closely with the other parts of the organization or unwanted consequences may be suffered, such as degraded organizational performance. Changing my brand of toothpaste impacts nobody

but me, and I can work the change anyway I want. This is not the case in a big organization where an uncoordinated change might have a disastrous ripple effect.

2. For a business organization that is operating effectively and efficiently in serving its customers and paying its stockholders, there are only a relatively small number of changes that can be made that will have a positive impact on the business. This second complicating factor really limits the degree of latitude you have in making certain kinds of changes. I could probably change to any one of a dozen brands of a given toothpaste and still be relatively satisfied. But for a business that is operating well in a highly competitive environment, there are only a few changes that can be made that will produce better results for the business—and the organization usually is not 100 percent sure exactly what those changes are. So any change is made with caution until the organization senses whether or not the change is a good one.

3. While people have grown up with a natural ability to change what they do and how they do it at a personal level, in organizations, *people have been trained not to change!* As children we are free learners and changers until we meet the organizations that we will live with for the rest of our lives. The first organization we encounter is a family that has a definite way of doing things—from regular bedtimes and rituals to the family's version of table manners. Children are encouraged to do things the family way without exception. In fact, parents have been known to be downright unreasonable about small things like innovation and creativity in table manners.

As we encounter our second big organization, school, we begin to get the message that there are a lot of things we are required to do, and not much tolerance is given to innovative new ways to do them. We quickly learn that schools are not interested in new ways for us to conduct ourselves in class or study hall. We are taught the exact way to write a term paper and even how and where to put our name on the title page. We begin to get the message that organization means stability, repetition, and standards—the very opposite of innovation and change.

As we enter the workforce, we usually enter an established company to take an existing job in an ongoing operation. Our first actions are to learn to do the job the required way and then to do it that same way every time thereafter. Here the concepts of policies, procedures, job descriptions, and organization charts are also added to our understanding of the nature of organizations. We are consciously taught ways of ensuring that things in an organization do not change, lest there be unwanted variation in product quality or customer satisfaction.

In short, our natural implicit capability to change comes in direct conflict with an organization's need to greatly limit change and variation. And the more an organization is fighting for resources in a highly competitive environment, the more change will be limited by the prudent management of that organization. For many of us, our first explicit lesson about organizational change is likely to be don't do it.

THE NEED TO MASTER CHANGE

So here we are, natural changers living in organizations that encourage us *not* to change because it might negatively impact the output of the organization. Over time we pick up more and more skills for controlling or limiting change. And if we are in one of many industries, we may have worked for years without encountering any significant organizational changes. We become long on tools for retaining stability and sameness and short on the tools that might be needed if organizations really began to encourage change.

And then what happens? Organizations begin to ask for more change because the competitive environment demands it and stakeholders want it! But the wanted changes still need to be well coordinated and within the zone of acceptable change. So here we are, faced with the need for organizational change, and, for the most part, missing the skills and tools needed to make that kind of change happen!

THE CURRICULUM FOR MASTERING CHANGE

After almost 30 years of working with managers and employees while they experienced change—either attempting to lead it or taking part in it—we have found that there are five change subjects that are clearly more important than others.

1. Understanding change
2. Leading change

3. Engineering change
4. Managing change
5. Mastering change

The critical content areas of those subjects are what make up the remainder of this book. Before we dive into the details of those subject areas, let's start with an overview of the curriculum for mastering change.

UNDERSTANDING CHANGE

The starting place for mastering change is with the understanding of what an organization is and what organizational change means. We are not implying that people who work in companies don't understand them—of course they do, to the level needed to do a good job of running their day-to-day business. But we have found that most managers and employees do not understand organizations at the level needed for organizational change. It would be hard to say that I don't understand my car; I drive it to work everyday, I ensure that it's taken care of, I even play with it occasionally on a deserted winding road. Of course I understand it—as a transportation system or a toy. But the truth is that I don't understand very much about my car as a mechanical system. I've always counted on somebody else to keep it running.

Mastering change requires us to know something about what an organization is from a structural or system point of view. To master change, we need to learn something about the mechanics of organizations, just as a driver would have to learn some mechanics if he had to take over responsibility for maintaining his car. In today's world of work, we must be able to both *use* the organization to get today's business done and to *change* the organization so that we can be ready to do tomorrow's business.

Understanding Organizations as Ongoing Theatrical Performances

We see an organization as an ongoing play where organization members are cast and crew in a satisfying performance for customers. We use the idea of changing the play from *Romeo and Juliet* to *My Fair Lady* as an example to depict what happens in organizational change.

Both managers and employees easily grasp the changes needed to move a theater company from one performance to another—from learning new scripts and parts to changing costumes and sets, all the way to the full dress rehearsal before opening. Once this theater metaphor is learned, our students of change management can easily use it to understand why many changes go awry!

Understanding Organizations as Mechanical Systems

Once the theater metaphor is mastered, it becomes easy to understand the single most important concept in organizational change: organizations are structured, mechanical systems with concrete moving parts that must work and change together. Organizations have four primary structural elements: (1) vision (like the play's storyline and script), (2) work processes (like the roles in the play), (3) plant/equipment/tools (like costumes and sets), and (4) performance agreements (like contracts for actors).

While it is easy to comprehend the work process–role and the plant/equipment–props connections, it does take some imagination to see that the performance agreements, like actor contracts, are an attribute of the organization and not the employees/actors themselves. In our experience, the most difficult part of organizational change for many companies is seeing that change is designed to alter the roles that people play in the organization, not to alter people themselves. Failure to grasp the idea that change hinges on altering roles and the subsequent performance agreements that we make with employees is the most common downfall of organizational change.

For an organization to change, all four mechanical attributes of the organization must change—in concert—or there will be no change. Vision alteration, work process alterations, plant/equipment/tools alterations as well as performance agreement changes are all done in a social setting. All the alterations have to be done by people who are involved and committed to making the alterations and working in the new organization after the alterations are made. Managing the people dynamics can be challenging, but it is doable as long as leaders of the change understand the mechanical things that must be done for organizational change.

Organizational Change as a
Competence for Everyone

Imagine an actor in a long-term production who discovers that the play will close, and that the theater company will move on to another performance. Imagine that actor having no idea about the need to find a role in the new play, to learn the script that goes with the new role, to get fitted for a costume, to learn his way around the new set and props, or to take directions from the director of the play to get ready for rehearsals! If you choose to be an actor, you better be ready and able to handle change! To be a manager or employee in today's business organization, you better be competent at change, or you will stand out like the one-role actor.

LEADING CHANGE

We look at organizational change as designed to make an organization stronger and better. When we talk about organizational change, we assume the organization is being changed by some members of the organization for some positive purpose. We believe that leadership is inseparable from organizational change. Leader roles exist in organizations to provide direction, energy, enthusiasm, and control. Providing that direction and energy brings change to the organization.

The Practical Role of
Leadership in Change

Leadership is a role that some have been selected to play. In today's business organization, there are many leadership roles, all designed to work together for the best interests of the organization. Another way to say it is that leadership is a required role in organizations, regardless of how many leaders there are. For successful organizational change, all those in leadership roles must accept the responsibility for both the direction of the organization and the results produced by the organization as it acts out that direction.

Accepting the responsibility of leadership requires taking personal and organizational risks. When the leadership of the firm does its job and identifies a future direction for the organization, it takes the risks that the organization will not change in that desired direction, and that the desired direction will not allow the organization to better meet its goals. But failure to take the risks is akin to doing nothing and letting the competitive business world determine the organization's results and future success. Imagine the theater director who is unwilling to risk a new production for fear that the seats will not fill! Holding on too long to the existing play is the certain recipe for unfilled seats!

The firm's leadership moves the organization forward by defining the future direction, sticking to that direction, and continuing to hold high the flag of that future direction so that the entire organization can move toward it in a coordinated way. Leadership's job is to hold the fort during the transition to the organization's future state. Imagine the theater director who loses his focus during the transition to the new play and begins to show his lack of confidence in the potential of the new play to fill seats! Or imagine the director becoming discouraged when the first rehearsal for the new play doesn't look like a Tony-winning performance! Leadership must be there with courage, confidence, and faith for organizational change to have even the slightest chance for success.

The Role and Value of a Change Vision to Complement Leadership

I cannot overemphasize the importance of a clear picture of the future, a vision, to guide organizational change. Without that single, clear picture, it would be impossible for the organization to be altered productively. Vision is the starting point for organizational change. Change happens as the attributes of the organization are altered in a coordinated way to meet the vision. That coordination is dependent on there being a single, understandable direction for the future. Imagine the theater company preparing for a future performance with the costume supervisor, the prop supervisor, and the acting coach each having a different play in mind! Worse yet, imagine them having only a title to the new play but no storyline or detailed script!

Different organizations describe the future they want to create in different terms. Some organizations use a vision as the guiding picture of the future they desire to create. Others use the concept of strategy, mission, purpose, or gameplan. The form of directional device is not important as long as one exists—and works!

Vision is the product of the leadership of the organization. And the vision must be supported by the entire leadership of the firm. That support must be unanimous and unwavering—and that's not negotiable! Imagine how the director of a play would handle things if the costume supervisor and the prop supervisor didn't like the new play and were unwilling to produce costumes and props that fit the new script!

Participation in the development of the vision for organizational change is important but not totally necessary. In fact, a participative decision about the vision may not produce the very best vision for the organization. It is up to the leadership of the firm to ensure a clear vision is present, whether it be the will of the majority or not. Imagine the theater director who refuses to select a new play until a majority of the cast and crew vote on which play they think will produce the best business results!

For organizational change to be successful, there must be a vision in place, and that vision must be both current and flexible. Visions can be revised over time as the leadership of the organization better assesses what is needed for future success. Imagine the theater director revising her plans for the look of the future play as reactions come in from the first performance. Flexibility of vision is also required as the organization deals with some physical constraints during implementation, such as a theater that agrees to host your play but lacks the room needed for your planned props.

THE FIVE REQUIREMENTS
FOR ENGINEERING CHANGE

The way any organization works at a given point in time is the direct and inescapable result of the configuration of the firm's vision, its work processes, its plant/equipment/tools, and its performance system (agreements with employees and their competence to perform to those agreements). Just as in a mechanical system, the way the organization operates cannot change without a change in its key components. So organizational change requires physical alteration of these four components or there will be no change at all. Calling these needed alterations *requirements* allows us to see change as a true engineering challenge! These four alterations, along with the development/communication of action plans, make up what we call the five requirements for engineering change. The critical part of organizational change is the unglamorous, detail-oriented, hard work of engineering!

Requirement One:
Engineering and Communicating
the Change Vision

The first requirement of organizational change is to engineer a vision of the organization's desired future that will be valid, complete, feasible, resourceable, and engaging. Once detailed, the vision should be tested with members of the organization to ensure that it is an understandable picture of the desired future. To ensure that the organization is positioned to really hear and digest the vision, we construct a case for change that describes in some detail the potential consequences of keeping the organization exactly the way it is now.

Once the change vision and the case for change are complete, the next needed step is to communicate with all organization members multiple times using multiple media. This requirement is not complete until all management levels have worked through the vision and case for change and translated them into action terms for their level and function, as well as for their individual players. The final step in this requirement is to test each employee's understanding of the translation of the vision for his or her job. Without this test, leaders of the change can hardly know if they are ready to move on to the next set of requirements to alter the mechanical components of the organization.

Failure to translate the vision and case for change would be like the director of a theater company who does not individualize the new play for each member of the cast and crew. Imagine trying to move to a new play without specific role assignments for each actor!

Requirements Two through Four:
Engineering the Organization's
Mechanical Components

Requirements two through four call for the physical alteration of work processes, plant/equipment/tools (PET), and the performance system. The first step in this alteration process is to inventory the organization's current components—work processes, PET, and performance agreements with employees—to identify those elements that will not be in sync with the vision of the future organization. Once identified, each of the elements must be physically altered and tested. It is these alterations of the existing components, along with the addition of new work processes, PET, and performance agreements that will become the *stuff* of the new organization.

Development and negotiation of new performance agreements for all affected managers and employees is critical at this point to ensure they are signed up for the new organization. Organizations and theater companies alike deal with the reality that some employees or actors will *not* elect to sign up for the change.

Completing these alterations is akin to the work that must get done in the theater company to ensure that the new play is translated into individual roles and scripts for the newly assigned cast, that the new costumes and sets have been constructed, and that the actors have been put under formal contract and rehearsed for the new play.

The final step in each of these three requirements is to systematically dismantle or remove those elements that will not be a part of the new organization's structure. Old work processes, procedures, tools, and equipment will need to be removed from the workplace to ensure they will not be used again. This dismantling includes the often forgotten step of directly and formally canceling any agreements with managers and employees for performance in the old organization. We are not talking about layoffs. We want to cancel the agreements that our employees had for doing work the old way now that they have already been signed up to do work the new way. This final dismantling is akin to the director removing all vestiges of the last play (old scripts, costumes, and props) to ensure that they will not be inadvertently used in the new production. Included in this dismantling step is the cancellation of any cast contracts that would have tied them to the old play.

Requirement Five: Engineering Action Plans for Change Work

Even though employees are clear on the vision that is to be implemented, they need day-by-day or week-by-week action plans to guide them through the many steps of organizational change. Employees need an action plan that tells them what to do on Monday morning to go forward with the coordinated implementation of the new vision.

These action plans must be a part of a critical path project management plan and master schedule that lays out all the engineering work to be done for the organizational change. Critical to the action planning requirement is the translation of action plans on a weekly or monthly basis for all involved managers and employees so that they are clear on both their roles in transitioning to the new organization as well as playing a new or altered role in that new organization. Failure to keep action plans up to date and communicated would be like the director who does not lay out and communicate detailed plans and schedules for the reading for new roles, signing of contracts, fittings for new costumes, or rigging of new props.

The engineering challenge in this action planning requirement is to ensure that all of the required modifications to vision, work processes, PET, and performance agreements have been done in a thorough and comprehensive manner. While it may be a technical challenge to keep track of all of the needed alterations, particularly if the organization is large, it is technically not difficult to find out exactly where the organization is in organizational change. Either identified work processes have been altered or they have not. Either the *new* PET is on board and working or it is not. Either the *old* PET has been removed and disabled or it has not. Either the performance agreements for each and every manager and employee impacted by the change have been altered and negotiated with them or they have not. Either each and every manager and employee has been trained on the new processes and new PET or they have not. And so on! The theatrical equivalent of this step is the director's periodic inventory of the transition to the new play: which actors are still not under new contract, which costumes have still not been completed, and which props are not yet scheduled for manufacture.

MANAGING CHANGE

Organizational change is a tough enough assignment by itself given so many moving parts—individual alterations to be made and performance agreements to be negotiated. Unfortunately, organizational change toward a new future is not the only thing the organization has to do. Besides change, the organization must continue to serve today's clients in a satisfactory way—and at a profit! The total amount of work for an organization simply must go up during organizational change or the organization will pay the piper in lost sales and profit or in a lack of change progress. The challenge to change leaders is the day-to-day management of the rate of change while continuing to ensure that today's customers are properly served and at the business-operated targeted profit level.

The theatrical example of this complex management task would be the company that is transitioning to a new play during the day while continuing to perform an old play to paying customers in the evening. The director's challenge would be to continue to satisfy the audience for the *old* play right through the last Saturday night performance and to put on an equally satisfying performance of the *new* play for the audience at the next day's matinee!

Running the Business
While Changing the Business

In organizational change in the real world of today's business, the organization is literally doing two things at once: (1) running the *present* business and (2) changing so that there will be a *new* way of doing business for the future. Doing these two things at once calls for everyone in the organization to take on the challenge of doing enough of both running and changing so that both things get done satisfactorily. Critical to this dual perspective or focus is for top management to take the lead in the changing of the business while other management takes the day-to-day lead in running the business. Also top management must ensure that the change vision stays in clear focus for the organization.

Doing two things at once requires two focal points or agendas that spell out the priorities for both running and changing the business. Each perspective should be guided with its own short list of goals, its own incentives, and its own management forums for checking progress. Finally, managers must use the business opportunities to provide the energy and focus for getting what appear to be the less-glamorous things on the change list done.

The theatrical equivalent here would be the director working with his second in command, who follows a gameplan to keep the present play winning every evening while systematically doing the transition work needed to prepare for the new play during the daytime. This is no simple challenge for a director or for an organization's leadership as it moves forward on both running and changing the business.

Managing Change Realistically

Top management must keep the throttles open for both running and changing the business while keeping in mind the organization's capacity. An organization can only do so much before it runs out of time and energy to do anything well. The manager's job is to keep an accurate, real-time assessment of the organization's change capacity and the limitations of the human beings involved.

The business world may have changed, but the capacity of our people has not. We still have our physical limits. People are capable of successfully working a list of seven to nine items, but they can't handle lists of 70! People can handle prioritized lists, but they can't handle a list where everything on the list is top priority. People can handle some ambiguity—in fact some ambiguity is stimulating—but they can't handle large amounts of it. Management's job is to control the throttles to ensure that the organization has the right amount of work and change to focus on. The director transitioning his cast and crew must keep in mind the physical limits of people—perhaps using more stand-ins for the evening performances of the old play so that the lead actors in the cast are fresh for the daytime rehearsals of the new play.

In addition, management must monitor organizational change to ensure that it is within reasonable bounds of the organization's identity. Not only does an organization have a change capacity limit from a time and energy point of view, but an organization may be limited in what it can become because of what it is and what it has been. Imagine a director attempting to transition his long-time cast and crew from a string of Shakespearean productions to a version of the big hit musical *Ragtime*!

MASTERING CHANGE

It is one thing to go through one or a series of organizational changes. It is another thing to really learn how to change in an effective and efficient manner, particularly if the goal is to learn to change our businesses on target, on time, and on budget. We must move organizations and individuals to a point where change expertise is as second nature as running their businesses.

The Organization Masters Change

Organizations must develop and institutionalize work processes that are devoted to change. Just as a traveling theater company develops systematic checklists for rigging up and rigging down in each new theater, organizations must have change checklists that capture hard-learned change lessons in a form that is easy for the organization to efficiently use. Organizations must have built-in methods devoted to designing organizational changes and the work processes that make them, reviewing and evaluating potential changes, implementating program and project management, and establishing controls to ensure that the configuration of the organization and its mechanical components does not change unless needed.

Just as a traveling theater company learns something from each performance in a new town or theater, the organization must learn something from each change and be able to add it to its overall change knowledge.

The Employee Masters Change

Just as organizations must learn change and install the change machinery needed to make change effective and efficient, people must also learn about organizational change. Most individuals go through many organizational changes during a work career and have the motive to learn. Managers and employees begin to learn change by accepting the reality of the workplace. No organization goes long without changing, just as no theatrical performance lasts forever!

At the heart of learning change for employees is the realization and acceptance of the fact that they are solely responsible for their work careers. Employees then learn that the way to make progress in their personal careers is to do everything in their power to cause their employing organization to win in the marketplace, just as actors learn that career progress happens with each great performance in their theater company's selected play.

Today's business world demands that organizations make frequent changes to stay competitive and strong. Right now, many organizational changes are being handled by managers and employees who have not learned to change effectively and efficiently. In fact, many of these organization members have been schooled in how not to change. The challenge is to master change, something that can be done with the right curriculum coupled with real-world change opportunities and experiences that teach valuable lessons. Only after organizations and individuals have really mastered change will we be able to truly change organizations on target, on time, and on budget.

AN IMPORTANT NOTE
FOR THE READER

My experience in teaching change has been that some managers prefer to dive into the detail of change while others want to see the big picture. Therefore, I have constructed the chapters so that you have optional paths through the book.

Option 1:
Diving into the Detail of Change

If it is the details you want, continue to read the remaining chapters in order. That order will lead to the detailed mechanics of change first (Chapters 2 through 8), followed by a big picture perspective on change in the context of running the business on a daily basis (Chapter 9: Running the Business while Changing the Business). You will finish this option with warnings about managing change realistically and guidance for developing change mastery (Chapters 10 and 11).

Option 2:
The Big Picture View
of Change Management

If it is the big picture you want, read Chapter 9 next (Running the Business while Changing the Business). That chapter will provide a high-level look at the essential nature and requirements of change management before the detailed mechanics of change in Chapters 2 through 8. After completing Chapter 8, you might review Chapter 9 to cement the idea that any organizational change must be made in the context of running the business. Then read Chapters 10 and 11 for guidelines for realistic change and change mastery.

Option 3:
"I Only Have Time to
Read One More Chapter"

Go straight to Chapter 9 to read the single most important chapter needed for mastering change, Running the Business while Changing the Business. Then when your organization heads toward the next big change, tackle the detailed change mechanics in Chapters 2 through 8 and the warnings and mastery guidelines in Chapters 10 and 11.

PART TWO

Understanding Change

We do not have good metaphors for understanding the simple mechanical components of organizations. Seeing organizations through the lenses of psychology and social science have not helped us understand the physical nature of organizations. Much of today's understanding of change leaves out the one model of organizations that could make change much more understandable. We have forgotten that organizations are first and foremost mechanical systems that call for engineering as well as art.

My underlying promise in this book is that the reader will be able to identify and use practical actions that lead to successful organizational change. I believe that practical actions are possible for all organizational change issues, if and only if, the change leader has a good understanding of the organization as a mechanical system.

2

Change as a Mechanical Process

To be able to make change happen, it is important to understand what an organization is and how it works. In our simple view, organizations are designed to use four components or moving parts to produce results. Results happen when (1) people, employees, use (2) a physical plant and tools in (3) work processes that produce products and services to serve (4) a purpose, direction, or vision for the organization. The way any organization works at a given point in time is the direct and inescapable result of the configuration of the firm's processes, its plant/ equipment/tools (PET), its performance systems, and its vision.

For example, a company decides that its purpose is to produce software that helps oil companies see underground, that is make three-dimensional computer pictures of the underground geological formation where oil companies might want to drill for oil. People in the software company use computer tools to go through a set of work processes that produce the software needed by oil patch clients to see formations underground.

We have taken this rather simple and straightforward description of the moving parts of an organization as the underpinning of our concept of mastering change. We have chosen these parts precisely because they are simple and relatively tangible things that managers can easily relate to. We have chosen to avoid many of the more sophisticated ideas of what organizations are, or should be, because those ideas make visualizing change more difficult. We do believe that ideas, like living organisms, learning organizations, socio-technical systems, and so on, do add value to our understanding of how organizations operate. But in many cases, they mask the simple mechanical features of organizations that managers need to see and manipulate in order to make change happen.

The purpose of this chapter is to allow the reader to grasp the simple mechanical features of organizations that I have found to be at the heart of practical actions for organizational change. I start by describing in some detail each of these four moving parts of an organization. I then show how organizational change happens when and only when these parts are altered. I will use simple doses of the theater metaphor to explain and illustrate the four parts of the organization in very simple terms.

UNDERSTANDING THE ORGANIZATION AS A MECHANICAL SYSTEM

By *mechanical* I mean concrete or tangible. Organizational moving parts like vision, work processes, PET, and worker contracts are mechanical—concrete and tangible. For example, the engine and the transmission are mechanical parts of the system of a car. These are concrete parts of a car as a system as opposed to the attributes of a car that we label as its feel, cachet, or snob appeal.

By *system* I mean that the moving parts of the organization are tied together interdependently. When one part of the organization is changed, the other parts of the organization must be correspondingly changed to allow the organization to keep its level of functioning. If a car driving at 30 mph is shifted into a lower gear, engine revs must be increased accordingly to keep the car at 30 mph.

Part 1:
Understanding Vision as
Story Line and Script

We have probably all been to a movie or theater production and come out with the evaluation that the plot was weak or even nonexistent. What we usually mean by that evaluation is that there was limited attractiveness, fun, or satisfaction. The production just didn't work for us. Many of us have also discovered that other theatergoers had the same reaction. Remember *Waterworld?*

Organizations also have a plot or story line that gets executed by the people in the organization. Sometimes it is a good story line (Windows software) and sometimes it is not (New Coke). Sometimes there is a great story line (Apple Computers) that is executed poorly.

Organizations use different words or terms to describe their story lines or plots. Story lines are called many things: mission, purpose, vision, strategy, gameplan, direction, or any one of a dozen other terms. The hottest new title for an organization's story line is the mind twister, value proposition. Our position is simple, we don't care what an organization calls its story line, it is just critical that the organization has one and knows what it is. Now lest we take too much heat from the careful and experienced readers of this book, we know that the terms mission, vision, etc., have very precise meanings and distinctions. In fact, we get a lot of consulting work helping our clients with these terms. Our interest and idea is again simple; when an organization wants to change, one of the four things it will need to modify or alter is its story line—whatever it is called.

For example, if the software company that I described earlier wants to serve customers other than the ones it has in the oil patch, the company's story line must be altered to include those new customers or there will likely be no shift from what the company is doing. Beyond the story line shift, the processes of the organization must be altered to now address and serve these added customers. Altering the processes will likely require a different mix of equipment and tools and altered assignment of worker roles to cover the new processes.

In a theater production, there is a high likelihood of a written script from which actors can read or conclude the story line. In organizations, much of the story line is not written down for anybody to read. Even in those cases where the organization has a written and posted mission, vision, and/or strategy, much of the story line is implicit—understood by many but not written down. In later sections of this book, I will make recommendations about making more of the organization's story line explicit to support organizational change initiatives. The bottom line is this: if you want the world to see a different story line from your organization, you will need to develop and detail that story line or you will have nothing to use as a target for an organizational change.

Part 2:
Understanding Organizational
Processes as Parts in the Play

Theatergoers can easily spot parts in a play because different actors do different things on stage. That is, each actor is seen taking certain steps, saying certain lines, interacting with other actors in certain scenes. And if the theatergoer were to return to the theater again, she would likely see the same actors doing those same things all over again. In organizational terms, the parts that actors play are the daily work processes that produce the organization's goods and services.

An observer could follow different workers in an organization to see or even document the steps taken by that worker over the course of a time cycle (a work day, week, or month). Following all the workers in an organization could theoretically allow the observer to see all of the organization's work processes. An observer who sees all of an organization's work processes is likely to conclude, in a well-managed organization, at least, that all the processes seem to be focused on bringing about the purpose of the organization.

For example, if we watch all the employees of that software company over a period of time, we would see work processes focused on identifying customers, determining what kinds of software they might need and be willing to buy, developing such software, producing and testing that software, and so on. Just as the parts in the play bring the story line to life, so do the work processes of the organization bring about the desired organizational purpose.

In fact, the results that are produced by any organization at a given point in time are directly related to both the kind and performance level of all of the organization's work processes. From an organizational change perspective, if we want customers to see a different story line, or a different way of doing business, we will need to modify or alter the organization's work process.

Part 3:
Visualizing Plant/Equipment/Tools as
the Theater/Props for Your Organization

Theatergoers see props and parts of a theater when they go to a performance. They don't see all of the theater or the behind-the-scenes props, but they assume they are there based on what happens on the stage. As scenes change, actors dangle from the ceiling, or run into and out of rooms or buildings. For many plays to make sense to the audience, certain props or costumes are needed. Imagine for a moment *Cats* being performed by actors in business suits! While props and costumes don't make the play, they clearly are indispensable parts of the whole, and the clarity of the story line would suffer without them.

Just like in the theater, organizations require the use of PET to execute the work processes needed to produce the products and services that fulfill the organization's purpose or direction. The computer software company uses office buildings, furnishings, communication equipment, and computer hardware and software to bring to life its work processes and to make possible the development and testing of its primary product: software for the oil patch.

And just as in the theater, some of an organization's PET are visible and some are invisible. Invisible tools include everything behind the walls, under the floor, and in the ceiling as well as what's inside the computer. Software turns out to be an indispensable tool in many of today's organizations, as all the Y2K concern showed us, and software is, to a large degree, invisible to most workers. For an organization to change the way it does business through its work processes, the organization's PET must be altered, whether they are visible or invisible.

Part 4:
Understanding Performance
Systems That Guide People
as Contracts and Training

We clearly see the actors when we go to the theater. It is the actors that bring the story line of the play to life. But what we see is the performance given by the actors. We know as we sit in the theater that the person we are seeing onstage is a professional acting her part and speaking her lines from the script. We also know that the actress is under contract to do the play, and that the performance we are seeing is only possible after this professional studies and rehearses her part.

We see workers in organizations as actors with assigned parts who are under a kind of contract to give a performance for the organization. We see the training that the worker has received as akin to the study and rehearsal done by the actor to be able to perform in a play. The workers in the software company have different roles in the organization calling on them to act in assigned work processes, like software development, while using the tools of the company to produce software products for customers.

The concrete, moving parts of the organization that we use in mastering change are worker contracts and training. We call these moving parts the *performance system* that leaders of an organization use to ensure that workers will do all the needed work for organizational success. In the theater, for example, the performance management system would be similar with specific contracts for actors (calling for a performance in an assigned role for a certain amount of compensation) and planned rehearsals to ensure that the actors have developed their parts and are able to perform as required.

Beyond the contract, the actor receives direction from the director on some of the finer points of the performance of the part. The director has the responsibility to tell the story in the play through the performance of the actors. And the actors have the responsibility to act their parts to the best of their ability to ensure a successful performance. In organizations, workers have the responsibility to act out their assigned roles with the assistance of a manager who is responsible for blending a number of roles into the performance needed to meet organizational goals.

THE ANATOMY OF ORGANIZATIONAL CHANGE

Just as in a mechanical system, the way the organization operates cannot change without a change in its key components or moving parts. Organizational change requires physical alteration of these components or there will be no change at all. Only by altering the real parts of the organization can change be successfully accomplished.

Critical Definitions

To get at the anatomy of organizational change, we need to begin with some basic definitions. You should keep in mind that our assumed context is one of planned change in which organizational leaders consciously plan to change the organization for the better. When we talk about the anatomy of change, it is in the setting of the work that employees will be exposed to:

- *Old Work.* This is the work that the organization and its workers currently do (i.e., today the company is making two product lines for two markets) until it is time to change over to a new way of operating. Using our theater metaphor, old work is performing the old play.

- *New Work.* This is the work that the organization and its workers will do after the changeover to the new way of operating (the new organizational vision) (i.e., new work is making three product lines for four markets). In theatrical terms, new work is performing the new play.
- *Change Work.* This is work that must be accomplished to enable the organization to change over to the new organizational vision (altering vision, altering work processes, altering PET, altering individual worker roles, holding contracting sessions, training workers, etc.). In theatrical terms, change work is the transition work needed to be able to perform the new play.
- *Changeover.* This is the act of stopping the old work and starting new work (starting to sell new product lines in new markets on a chosen date). In theatrical terms, changeover is opening night for the new play.
- *Change Leader(s).* This is the individual (or set of individuals) who has the primary responsibility and accountability for moving the organization from doing old work to doing new work. Change leaders are responsible for ensuring that the needed change work is done—on target, on time, and on budget. In theatrical terms, the primary change leader is the director of the new play.

Organizational change is now relatively simple to describe when we use our change definitions. For example, the leaders in an organization want to change the way the company is currently doing business (old work) in order to make more money (or serve clients better.) Key executives (change leaders) decide how they want the organization to do business in the future (the vision of organizational change). They then decide how the various parts of the organization will need to be modified/altered (change work) in order to be able to do work the new way. They then set out to make those required alterations (change work) while the organization continues to serve existing customers the current way (old work). Once the needed alterations are completed, leaders authorize workers to begin doing things the new way (changeover to new work).

Figure 2.1 shows change work being done while old work is still going on. Doing both at the same time is an absolute requirement of successfully changing an organization on target, on time, and on budget. Many organizations have learned the hard way that the other ways of sequencing change work are disastrous. Stopping old work, doing change work, than changing over to new work produces a long period

FIGURE 2.1 The Anatomy of Change

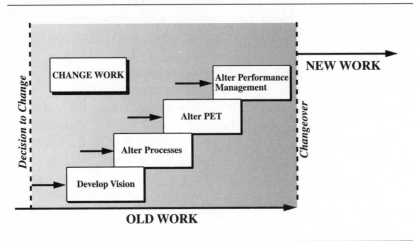

of time when products don't get produced and customers don't get served. Changing over to new work before change work is done results in poor, or no, product production or customer service. Imagine the theater director who announces the new play, then yells, "Show time! We'll rehearse and fit costumes live in front of our paying customers!"

The Categories of Change Work

There are four categories of change work that must be done for an organization to change from old work to new work. We describe each kind of change work as an alteration to one of the four mechanical parts of the organization. We use the idea of alteration because our subject is organizational change, that is, changing an existing organization in which there already exists each of the four kinds of organizational moving parts.

1. *Altering Vision.* This kind of change work is focused on envisioning (or designing) the way the organization should get work done after the change so that the organization's goals of making things better can be met. If changes to old work are to be minor, we alter the current vision to make it the vision of new work. If changes are to be major, we might want to develop a new vision from scratch. In the theater, altering the vision can be anything from leaving out a song or two to shorten the production or changing a relatively serious story line to a spoof.

2. *Altering Work Processes.* This kind of change work is focused on changing the steps in the organization's work processes so that those processes will have a different outcome. Altering work processes could mean adding steps to the work process of finding prospects or changing steps in another process. Altering work processes frequently means eliminating steps that had been taken in the past to reduce cost or complexity. In theater, altering roles could mean anything from moving the responsibility for opening a door to moving lines from one actor to another.

3. *Altering PET.* This kind of change work is focused on changing from one kind of work equipment to another, or performing some kind of technical modification on existing equipment to give it different capabilities Altering PET could mean changing to a different kind of software or adding a new application to an existing computer system. In theater, altering PET could mean anything from freshening the set with a new coat of paint to making major set/prop alterations to fit the performance into a new theater.

4. *Altering Performance Management.* This kind of change work is focused on changing the roles that people play in the organization by adding or eliminating the responsibility to perform steps in work processes. Altering performance management will also mean adjusting the compensation agreement so that the worker will be compensated for the new role and not for the old one. Altering the performance system will likely include training for the worker on those aspects of his new role that are unfamiliar or that have skill requirement different from his current skill set.

THE VARIETY OF ORGANIZATIONAL CHANGES

It is quite common to hear managers talk about many different kinds of organizational changes—and there are many! For mastering change, however, we have found that almost all kinds of organizational change can fit into one of the four categories below. The four garden varieties of change are:

1. *Strategy Change.* This is a change brought about by the need to shift a company's direction or competitive strategy. Compaq Computer decided to shift its competitive strategy (the way it

presented itself in the market place) from differentiation to being the low cost producer in a rapidly expanding PC market.

2. *Process Change.* This is a change brought about by the need to modify some of the ways an organization is doing its business. IBM made changes in its credit processes with customers in order to allow faster processing time of applications and approvals for credit purchases.

3. *System/Tool Change.* This is a change brought about by the installation of new equipment, a new plant, new hardware, or new software. Boeing implemented extensive 3-D automated design capability for the development of its major new wide body transport, the Boeing 777. The new capability allowed engineers to fit all the pieces together on the computer rather than with an extensive set of physical models.

4. *Cultural Change.* This is a change brought about at the behavioral level of managers and employees who need to have new skills or mindsets, or who need to operate in a new culture. GE's move to "six sigma" quality started as a shift in mindset and skills of employees aimed to dramatically change the level of product quality.

Regardless of the kind of change being pursued by the organization, all four mechanical components of the organization must be altered to enable each change. Once a change leader masters the alteration of the four mechanical parts of an organization, she should be able to effect change of any type. She will be working with the same four organizational mechanical parts in each change, but working with them in a slightly different order.

For example, while Compaq Computer's starting place for the change to become a low-cost producer was at the strategy level, to get the change made, alterations were required first in work processes, then tools, and then in the incentives and skills of workers. GE's culture change to six sigma quality also required the development of a new vision for the organization's operation, then altered worker incentives and skills, followed by altered processes and tools.

THE SOCIAL CONTEXT
OF THE ORGANIZATION
AS A MECHANICAL SYSTEM

Once an organization is formed, the people involved begin to act out their roles in concert with other organizational members. In the course of working together, either individually or as teams, people develop sentiments or feelings about what they are doing and whom they are doing it with. Workers discover that they like or dislike parts of the work and the workforce. It is clearly fair to say that an organization is a social system as well as a mechanical system.

My point in this book's approach to mastering change is not that organizations aren't social systems as well as mechanical ones, but that for organizational change to happen on target, on time, and on budget, the starting place is with the mechanical attributes of the organization and not with the social attributes.

Imagine a director who knows that a new play is needed—ticket sales are dropping by the week—but who starts the move to the new play by asking the actors if they are ready to move from the roles they have come to love. Imagine that director saying to the investors behind his theater company, "I don't think we can make a move to a new play any time soon. The actors love this play so much that it would upset them to change." Or imagine the director saying, "I have conducted a change readiness assessment and concluded that the current state of the organization would not allow a successful change at this time." It is interesting that comments like these would not be acceptable to theater folks, yet we hear such things all the time in other organizations.

An experienced director launches the move to the new play based on knowledge of the theater market, and he handles the change with great care and respect for the actors who might be moving to roles that don't at first seem to fit their tastes. He has respect for the organization as a social system of people who like and dislike each other, or who like or dislike the current play, but he makes his first moves by selecting the new story line (the new play), assigning new roles, getting the actors under new contracts and into rehearsal all while working in light of the social nuances of who likes whom and so on.

It is all too common today to see organizational change tactics focusing first on social attributes with secondary emphasis, at best, on the tangible mechanical components I have been describing.

MIND-CLEARING EXAMPLE

Imagine the director of a theater company who makes no plans for the physical transition of his company from the present play to the new one he wants to perform. Imagine there are no arrangements or schedules for passing out new scripts, for producing new sets or costumes, or for securing the services of the actors for the new play. Imagine that the director's primary tool for working on the transition was "town hall" meetings of all theater company members to talk about the change and to air their feelings and concerns about the transition. (Don't laugh! We have seen business organizations try to change exactly like this! And when the changes didn't work, they held more town hall meetings to allow workers to air their frustrations!)

CLARIFYING REAL-WORLD ORGANIZATIONAL CHANGE ISSUES

This chapter is all about building understanding of organizations and organizational change. By now, you should be able to use the basic definitions I have provided along with the theater metaphor to better understand the real-world change issues or problems that managers and workers face in today's work environment. Test your understanding of change mechanics in each one of the following common organizational change issues. Remember the metaphor of the theater company that is changing from the production of *Romeo and Juliet* to, let's say, *Grease*. Beyond better understanding each issue, you should be able to see ahead to the practical actions that would bring resolution.

Issue 1:
The Unclear Vision of the Future

- *Situation.* A department head complains that his workers keep asking for clarification of the upcoming change he plans for his organization. He is tired of dealing with all their questions and can't understand why they can't see things clearly. After all, he was in several days of planning meetings for the change and things are clear to him! "What do I do to get them back on track?" he asks the coach.

- *Translation for Practical Action.* The change coach says to the department head, "Now let me get this straight, Mr. Director. You're directing your company in the performance of *Grease,* but you haven't passed out the script you want them to use. If fact, you seem to resent their asking for one. And you, Mr. Director are asking me what you might need to do about it? Hand out the script! Describe the vision of how you want the organization to be operating in the future, and use your employees' questions to guide the level of detail you put in your description."

Issue 2:
The Equipment Is Not Ready for the New Work

- *Situation.* A department head hears that her workers are upset about the limits of the equipments' capabilities to help them perform what the new work process calls for. She finds them jury-rigging the equipment and asks them to explain. "We gotta get the work out and this is the only way we can get it done. When do we get the new equipment we need?" The department head seems in a quandary about what to do, and asks her change coach about the direction she should take.
- *Translation for Practical Action.* The change coach says to the department head, "Now let me get this straight. Your actors are on stage for *Grease* wearing Shakespearean costumes, acting out *Grease* with props from Juliet's balcony, and you, Ms. Director, want to know why they are upset? Get in gear and arrange for those tools—now!!"

Issue 3:
The Employee Is Not on Board

- *Situation.* A department head laments the fact that Charlie, one of his most dependable workers, has not yet embraced his organization's most recent change. The worker is complaining daily about the pressure he is feeling to change his ways and keeps saying that "it's his job, and he will do it his way!" The department head seems in a quandary about what to do, and asks his organization change coach about the direction he should take.

- *Translation for Practical Action.* The coach says to the department head, "Now let me get this straight. Charlie is walking onto the stage of your *new* performance of *Grease* still wearing his Romeo costume and singing the love songs to Juliet. When pressed about it, he says that it's his role and he'll handle it any way he wants! 'Besides,' he says, 'I think I look particularly good in these tights!' And you, Mr. Director, are asking me what you might need to do about it? It's time for a short and sweet conversation with Charlie: 'Are you in this play or not?' "

Issue 4:
Work Process Confusion

- *Situation.* Workers have been observed handling customers in different ways after the organizational change. Customers complain that their service level from the organization is uneven and haphazard. The workers each tackle their assigned jobs in different ways because each of them has his or her own idea about the definition of good customer service. The workers complain that they keep bumping into each other as they go about their own way of servicing customers. The department head seems confused about what to do, and asks her organization change coach about the direction she should take. "I'm just trying to allow some participation," she laments.

- *Translation for Practical Action.* The Coach says to the department head, "Now let me get this straight. You are allowing each member of your cast to choose his or her own song? You've got 'Beauty School Dropout' and 'Greased Lightening' being sung at the same time? And you, Ms. Director, are asking me what you might need to do about it? Look at your story line and decide which songs need to come in what order to maximize the overall impact on the audience. Then put all the actors on the exact same sequence of songs at the same time. Ask for input and participation about the sequence decision; but once that decision is made, ensure that it is enforced."

Issue 5:
The Uncommitted Boss

- *Situation.* A department head is tired of being bugged by his assistant department head about employee requests for the boss to show up and be a part of the planning for the upcoming organizational change. The department head asks the change coach why in the world the employees just can't accept the assistant as his representative during the planning for the new play.
- *Translation for Practical Action.* The coach says to the department head, "Now let me get this straight, Mr. Director. Your theater company has the unmitigated gall to ask you to be personally present to talk about the upcoming play? How dare they want to see the guy who is supposed to be behind this move to a new performance? And you, Mr. Director are asking me what you might need to do about it? Show up! Be the leader! Show your support! Your actions will speak far louder than your words!"

Issue 6:
On-Again, Off-Again Change

- *Situation.* A department head hears some of her workers complaining about *change de jour,* and gets upset about the possibility of poor morale in her department. She says that every time she talks out loud about how they need to change the organization, some of the workers think she is serious and begin to think about the upcoming change. The department head seems mystified about the situation, and asks her change coach what to do.
- *Translation for Practical Action.* The change coach says to the department head, "Now let me get this straight. Your company thinks there is an impending move to another play simply because you, the director, talk about it? You can't imagine why they would listen to you, the woman who is responsible for picking any new play to be done by the company. And you, Ms. Director, are asking me what you might need to do about it? Pick a play and stick with it! When it is time to consider a new play, label your considerations as analysis or evaluation of options, but don't keep talking about the next play without interpretation and context!"

Issue 7:
Confusion about the Transition Plan

- *Situation.* A department head gets frustrated when his employees keep asking about the schedule for training for the new organization. They also want to know when they are to learn about the new equipment they see being installed in their part of the facility. They keep asking when they are supposed to do what, and the department head asks the coach what he can do to quiet things down.
- *Translation for Practical Action.* The coach says to the department head, "Now let me get this straight, Mr. Director. Your theater company wonders when they are to show up for the fittings for their *Grease* costumes. They also think they have the right to know when rehearsals will be held and you are asking me what you might need to do about it? It's your job to schedule training and to give a reasonable timetable for the other activities your company will need to engage in to get fully ready for the new play!"

My contention in this book is that most of what a change leader needs to know is simple and straightforward. We don't need elegant theory to guide day-to-day change management, just a little knowledge of an organization as a mechanical system, a passing understanding of the theater metaphor, and some common sense!

PART THREE

Leading Change

The concepts of *change* and *leadership* are inseparable. Leadership is all about building organizations or businesses. Leadership is defined by the creative act of bringing new direction and, therefore, change to an organization.

3

The True Role of
Leadership

MIND-CLEARING EXAMPLE

Imagine how successful a theater company would be in transitioning to another play if the director were unwilling to name the new play. Or if he only said, "It's a musical." Worse yet, imagine that director announcing one play, handing out the script, and then, before anyone had time to digest the new play, changing to still another play!

At its heart, organizational change is an act of leadership. The role of the leader is to define a better future for the organization and then lead the organization to that future. Another way to say it is the leader's primary calling is to continue to grow the business for the better—in size, in vitality, in strength, or all three. This calling means that the leader will always be involved in leading in three fundamental ways: (1) leading today's organization to successfully serve its current customers (old work), (2) envisioning a new future for the organization that is better than this one (new work), and (3) leading the transition that goes on intermittently as the organization moves to that new future (change work). The focus of this chapter is the leadership that is required for change work.

Fortunately, the organization's chief executive does not have to work alone in organizational change. She has collaborators who also take initiative and demonstrate the leadership that is needed to move the organization to a better future. The organization's cadre of managers is also responsible for change leadership. Its daily focus may be on running today's business, but in times of change, the management cadre forms the arms and legs of the organization's change initiatives. Likewise, the organization's workers must take on the personal responsibility for altering their roles to fit with the vision of organizational change. Together these three sources of change leadership provide the true leadership needed in organizational change.

Organizational change does not happen without leadership—and lots of it! We have not seen success in change when the organization's leadership at all levels was unwilling to take responsibility for setting a direction or was lacking the courage and commitment needed to carry out that direction. Decisive leadership at the highest level of the organization is essential for successful change. The leader who is unable or unwilling to pick a new future for the organization, give that future some detail, and then steer toward that future is destined to keep her organization right where it is. Nor have we seen success in those organizations where the majority of managers were not willing to exercise leadership for change. Last but not least, we have not seen success where the vast majority of workers were unwilling to accept any responsibility for change. The bottom line is simple: organizational change takes leadership from both the boss and her collaborators. The final word, however, is that the boss must be the one who brings the energy and excitement to organizational change along with the personal leadership to get her collaborators on board.

THE ROLE OF LEADERSHIP IN ORGANIZATIONAL CHANGE

 MIND-CLEARING EXAMPLE

Imagine the producer/director who asks her cast and crew to move to a new play, but then takes no action. She does not hand out the script to the cast. She does not decide which actors go into which roles. She does not give any guidance to the costume designer for costumes and she gives no guidance to the designer about the kinds of props or sets that will be needed.

The role of leadership in organizational change is *action*. As illustrated in Figure 3.1, leadership acts on the four mechanical attributes of organization: (1) vision (script), (2) process (roles), (3) PET (set and costume), and (4) performance system (contracts and training). Unless the leadership of the organization takes firm, positive action, the organization's mechanical attributes will not be altered to facilitate the organizational change.

FIGURE 3.1 Change Leadership Acts on the Mechanical Attributes of Organizations

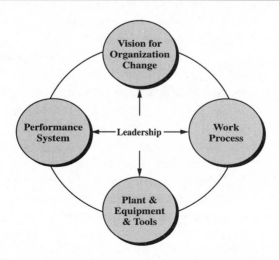

THE THREE SOURCES OF LEADERSHIP IN ORGANIZATIONAL CHANGE

 MIND-CLEARING EXAMPLE

Imagine the theater company preparing for a new production with only the director taking concrete action. Imagine the costume and set designers taking no initiative to produce new costumes and sets. Imagine the actors taking no initiative to learn their parts or to develop their roles. Imagine the stage manager taking no action to reserve the theater for the upcoming play!

In Chapter 2, we talked about leadership for change being a top down exercise. Well, it is, but the chief executive is not the sole leader of change. Not only does organizational change take a lot of leadership, it takes leadership from a lot of different folks! In fact everyone in an organization that is changing must exert some leadership—take some positive initiative—or the organizational change will not happen!

There are three critical sources of leadership that must be engaged for successful organizational change. Each leadership source has a primary mission to accomplish in organizational change.

1. *The senior executive is the chief change officer for the organization.* Period. No one else in the organization has the authority and stroke to make change happen. No one else has the legal responsibility for the enterprise. No one else can be held accountable for the performance of the organization before, during and after organizational change. The primary change mission for the chief executive in organizational change is defining the future for the organization.

2. *The cadre of management serves as the organization's source of energy and initiative for altering work processes, altering PET, and altering the performance system.* The primary change mission for the cadre of management is in the direction and leadership of the workers in organizational change. Like the director of the play, the managers of the company in change are the ones

that provide the day-to-day direction needed to ensure their parts of the organization's transition from old work to new work.

3. *The workers (nonmanagement) in the organization will do the majority of the change work that is needed to alter the organization's mechanical attributes.* It is the workers who will physically do the detailed alterations needed in work processes, PET, and in developing the new organizational roles that enact the change. The primary change mission of the workers must, however, be focused on the alteration and development of their own roles and skills needed for success in the new work of the organization.

Figure 3.2 shows many of the responsibilities that the different leaders must take to ensure that the mechanical attributes of the organization are altered for organizational change. The remainder of this chapter will focus on the primary change mission of each leadership source.

FIGURE 3.2 Workforce Responsibilities for Organizational Change

Sources of Change Leadership

		The Senior Executive	The Cadre of Managers	The Workers
Organization Attributes	**Vision for Change**	▶ Development or Selection of Vision for Change Communicating Vision to Cadre of Managers	Developing Unit Vision of Change Communicating Visions to Workers	Assimilating Vision of Organization and Unit Change
	Work Processes	Resourcing the Vision for Change	▶ Directing Workers in Process Alterations	Altering Work Processes
	Plant/ Equipment/ Tools	Resourcing the Vision for Change	▶ Directing Workers in PET Alterations	Altering PET
	Performance Management	Directing Cadre of Management Developing Personal Executive Role	▶ Directing Workers in Role Alteration Developing Personal Management Roles	▶ Developing Personal Worker Roles

▶ = Primary Change Responsibility or Mission

THE CHANGE MISSION OF
THE CHIEF EXECUTIVE:
DEFINING THE FUTURE

 MIND-CLEARING EXAMPLE

Imagine a director who picks a play that no one else likes—
neither the theater company nor the audience! Imagine a director who proposes a script for a new play that the theater company immediately sees as impossible to perform on the stage.
Or imagine the company receiving a new script that is so full
of inconsistencies and gaps that they are incapable of finding,
much less following, any kind of plot or story line!

The change mission of the chief executive is critical for successful
organizational change. The chief executive's primary change mission
is to

- develop (or select) the desired future for the organization and
  express it as the vision for organizational change,
- resource, with dollars and personal commitment, the vision as it
  is being implemented, and
- develop her own altered executive role as it will need to be played
  in the vision of organizational change.

Developing the Vision
of Organizational Change

The chief executive's primary mission in change is to select a future
vision for her organization that will sell to customers, investors, and
employees, just like the director's job is to select a script that will result
in a successful play. Then, as a theater director would bring the new
script to life for a theater company that is currently performing the old
play, the chief executive's job is to create that future for her current
organization.

The bottom line in both business and the theater is "the bottom line."
Businesses that don't make money over the long haul are thought of as

poorly as plays that can't draw an audience and, therefore, can't make money. Critical to the desired bottom line is a vision of a future that will work, that will please customers, and that will make money. The ultimate success of an organizational change will be measured by the success the organization has after it changes!

The chief executive's job is to define or select a successful future for his organization. The leader's job is to define a challenging but realistic future for his organization—to develop a vision of the future organization. You are probably familiar with the word *vision* as used by many managers today. The typical meaning of the word is "someplace the organization wants to be in the future." In this book, I will use vision in a more precise sense to mean "how we want an organization to look *after* an organizational change." In the traditional sense, vision usually applies at the organization-wide level as a part of defining a company's overall direction in its marketplace.

In this book, I will use *vision of organizational change* (VOC) to describe the desired end of an organizational change regardless of the size or scope of the change. Regardless of the type of change, we need to have a VOC that describes how we want and expect the organization to operate after the change. And that VOC will be constructed very much like the script of a play. In a script, we read about individual characters (employees) in an organizational structure who act out their roles (perform the work of the organization) using costumes and props (PET) to give the full effect of the plot of the play (meet organizational objectives). More will be said about the details of the actual construction of the VOC in Chapter 4. In this chapter, our goal will be to describe the attributes that a good vision should have to be a platform for organizational change.

Required attributes of a vision for organizational change. As a part of understanding the future vision, employees automatically evaluate the vision in terms of "goodness of fit" and logic. They subjectively check out the vision as a part of their process of deciding whether or not they should be willing to follow it. In short, employees need the vision to make sense to them, to paint a picture of someplace they would like to go, and someplace they can get to without totally upsetting their apple carts.

When we work with companies to engineer their visions, we keep several criteria in mind for shaping a vision that will have a high likelihood of being first understood and then eventually implemented. Details of the criteria that have worked the best for us follow.

The vision cannot be effective if it is not *valid, complete, possible, resourceable, and compelling.* At first glance, these five criteria seem pretty sophisticated. How are employees supposed to judge whether these five criteria are met? The answer is surprising: "We don't know, but they do!" When any of us hear about a new organization or a new product, don't we automatically conclude, "That will work. I would buy one!" or "That will never work. No way!" The point is simple. If a leader wants an organization to move toward a new future, that new future must be logical and make sense in each of the five identified areas.

A valid vision: Imagine the impact on a theater company that reads a script and concludes, "This will never sell. Nobody will want to see this!" Imagine the director hearing the same reaction from the audience after a trial performance. Imagine the trouble the director is in for when he insists that the company go forward with the new play anyway.

Employees must conclude that the VOC describes a new way of operating that will work, that will attract customers, and that will be a good business model. We want to implement a new direction that is valid—one that will be a good pattern for company success. A positive direction would be one in which:

- customers will be served and will want to come back for more,
- profits will be made and investors will want to invest even more,
- employees will be well paid, in both monetary and nonmonetary terms and will want to stay, and
- competitors will be held at bay.

If you are a leader who wants to move the organization toward a better future, you better take the time to make your picture of the new organization valid or employees will discount, disregard, or be apathetic toward your vision.

A complete vision: Imagine the impact on a theater company that reads a script and concludes, "This looks OK, but something's missing. The theme makes sense, but where is all the dialog? We don't have enough texture to get a real feel for the play!" Or, "Where is the last act? This script leaves us hanging. Is there a big ending or not?" Imagine the trouble the director is in for when she insists that the company go forward with the new play.

We want a VOC that is complete and worded so that a complete message is understandable to the organization. For a vision to be useable for engineering an organizational change, it must contain detailed information about where the leaders want the organization to be at a future time and information about the means to get there, including the high-level organizational structure that is to be in place after the change.

Complete also means that our VOC is stated in terms of concrete, precise goals/objectives for organizational performance in the targeted year. Goals and objectives are the language of organizations, and people are unlikely to judge a vision as complete unless they see these familiar indicators of organization direction.

A *possible vision:* Imagine the impact on a theater company that reads a script and concludes, "We'll never be able to pull this off. This is a stage production, not a George Lucas movie!!" Imagine the trouble the director is in for when he insists that the company go forward with the new play.

Managers are taught to communicate the future in ambitious terms. We are taught to set goals that are challenging and objectives that stretch the organization. Those key ideas are certainly useful in helping organizations become more effective and efficient. But they were meant to apply to people who were in jobs and organizations that they understood. They were meant to inspire innovation around the present organization and job structure to produce possible increases in performance. Frequently, we see these good challenging and stretching ideas applied wrongly in organizational change. For a vision to be useful in organizational change, it needs to be shaped as possible to achieve if organization members are to be able to use it to guide their behavior. Challenge around a known situation is very different than asking someone to form a crisp mental picture of something he or she doesn't think is possible.

The simple truth is that if people don't believe something is possible, most of them won't spend any time thinking about it. And they surely won't spend any time making plans to get to some place they don't think anyone can get to! The bottom line here is simple; wait until the change is made to the new organization and then come out with the ambitious, stretching goals to inspire performance to the next level.

A *resourceable vision:* Imagine the impact on a theater company that reads a script and concludes, "This play would take a fortune to stage. No backer will ever put enough money in this thing to do it right. And if it isn't done right, it won't come across right!" Imagine the trouble the director is in for when she insists that the company go forward with the new play.

For a vision to be useful for guiding an organizational change, the members of the firm must see how the firm will get the money, time, and people to put it into effect. If the members conclude that there is not enough time for implementation or for the market to respond to the envisioned organization, they will discount the vision. If the vision takes investment of capital that the members believe is unobtainable, the vision will be discounted. And if the vision includes people not now in the organization that will be very difficult to find or recruit, the vision will not be believable.

A compelling vision: Imagine the impact on a theater company that reads a script and concludes, "There is no real reason to do this play; the plot is outdated, no one will relate." Or "Why is a top-notch theater company like ours doing this amateur script? We need world-class challenges!" Imagine the trouble the director is in for when he insists that the company go forward with the new play.

The vision must be seen as appealing and attractive or most people will not be inclined to put much energy into thinking about it! The simple fact is that people need to be positively attracted to the work and the future of the organization or boredom and apathy will likely be a consequence. We human beings need to see ourselves getting ahead rather than falling behind. If our VOC doesn't offer a more prosperous future for both the company and its individual members, that vision will not be compelling. And if we are *not* going to propose a vision of greater success, why change the organization in the first place?

We have all seen tough times in our respective industries. It may seem like it's impossible to write a compelling vision for a firm going through bad industry times, but it can be done. In fact, we have seen organizations brightened considerably during tough times by a leadership team with a vision that includes how they are going to get through the tough times and prosper!

Beyond these five attributes, selecting or developing a VOC is risky. There is always a chance that a new organizational vision will not be one that is liked by the customers, just as a new play may not be liked by audiences. But taking that risk is part of the executive's job. After all, that's why she is paid the big bucks! Taking a risk may not be fun, but think about the long-term risk the executive takes by not taking the short-run risk associated with her VOC.

MIND-CLEARING EXAMPLE

Imagine the director of a play saying, "We obviously need to move to a different play, but I'm not sure which one might have the best chance of success. So we're going to blend several of the big successes into one play—*Oklahoma, Rent, Cats,* and *Lion King.* How could we fail with that?"

Executives cannot dodge the risk. They must accept it, assess the potential rewards that could come from change, and then manage the risks to the best of their abilities (I will say more about aggressive risk management in Chapter 8).

Resourcing the Vision
of Organizational Change

MIND-CLEARING EXAMPLE

Imagine the key assistants coming to the director with their needs for different costumes or scenery and hearing the director saying, "That's your problem. I've announced the new play. You go get the play ready." Imagine the stage manager saying, "Some of the actors are feeling uncomfortable about the play's chances of success and they want to hear again how we are going to pull this thing off." And the director replying, "Well, at the time, I thought we had selected a good play for our next run. But, who knows? Why don't you chat with them and see if they would be more comfortable with another play."

I mentioned earlier about the need to select or develop a VOC that is resourceable by the organization. Even if that gets done during the planning for organizational change, resourcing still comes up as a key part of the executive's change mission for several reasons. First, resources that were once committed for changing the organization have a way of becoming uncommitted. As the current business situation changes—and it always does—pressures are applied from many parts of the organization to use resources committed to change for other purposes. It is up to the chief change officer to keep those resources committed, by statement, by emphasis, or by finding alternate sources.

The second reason for the need to continuously resource the change initiative is that change is difficult, frustrating, and tiresome. Frequently, the chief executive will need to be the one that shows the flag and that personally holds the fort. It is critical for the chief executive to be personally visible and available while the organization is completing the change work needed to enact the VOC. The chief executive needs to be the rock in the face of the uncertainty of change. Many times we have seen an organization in change strengthened by the presence of a calm and confident leader who speaks positively about the future of the organization.

The third reason for the need to continuously resource the change initiative is that the change will never quite go as planned. Despite an organization's best efforts, things will happen that are unexpected: new work processes won't work the way they were supposed to, new equipment doesn't perform as advertised, customers won't react to new products or services the way they were expected to, employees learn new skills faster than expected, and so on. The chief executive must be there for the organization, continuing to make decisions and taking the initiative needed to keep the change momentum in place. It is during these times of uncertainty that the chief executive is the catalyst for action, gathering her troops around her and saying, "Ok, folks, let's put our heads and hands together to figure out how we are going to get through this latest obstacle, and then, let's do it!"

Developing the Personal Executive Role

 MIND-CLEARING EXAMPLE

Imagine the director announcing a new play to his theater company and then concluding that he would do his job exactly the same as he did in the last play, even though the new play is a real change for the company and a number of the actors will be playing very different kinds of roles!

Show me a chief executive who behaves the same way after her organization changes over to a new way of operating and I will show you an organization that probably has not really changed at all! Key to any significant organizational change effort is the time and energy spent by the chief executive in figuring out how she will play in the future, both in her executive role in new work after changeover and during the time when her organization is preparing for changeover.

We all know that actions speak louder than words, but we are talking about something more than that. What the chief executive does on a day-to-day, week-to-week, and month-to-month basis must change with the move to the new organization. Some or all of the following behaviors will need to change for the chief executive:

- How he describes the organization's future to customers, investors, and employees.
- The way he approaches or solves the organization's business problems.
- Whom he spends his time with in the organization.
- What parts of the organization will be resourced and what parts will not.
- Which customers he visits and what he talks about with them.
- The kinds of internal projects he visits and watches.
- His day-to-day language and vocabulary.

Unfortunately, this personal alteration of the executive role during organizational change is not given as much time and attention as we would like. Frequently, it is our job as consultants to coach organization members to say to the boss, "We hear you wanting the organization to change, but we see you still doing exactly the same things you were doing before the change."

THE CHANGE MISSION OF THE CADRE OF MANAGEMENT: DIRECTING THE CHANGE

 MIND-CLEARING EXAMPLE

Imagine the key assistants to a director listening politely to her announcement of the decision for a new play. Then imagine those key assistants taking no initiative to "get going" on the preparation for that new play; the costume manager, set designer, and stage manager all sit with hands folded over the next few weeks while the director scurries around trying to make things happen.

The organization's cadre of managers is directly and personally responsible for completing change work—on target, on time, and on budget. Just as it is unthinkable for the set designer to take no actions in the design of a new set, it is also unthinkable that the organization's entire cadre of managers would not be active leaders in the change effort. The cadre's job is to be the chief change communicator and director for its part of the company. The primary change mission of the cadre of management is to

- communicate the vision for organizational change,
- direct the workers as they complete the organization's change work, including the development of their roles, and
- develop its own altered management roles as they will need to be played in the VOC.

Communication of the Vision
of Organizational Change

 MIND-CLEARING EXAMPLE

Imagine the key assistants to a director listening politely to her announcement of the decision for a new play. Then imagine those key assistants taking no initiative to communicate the director's ideas as well as their own to the other members of the theater company. Imagine the stage manager saying, "I just manage the show; any questions about what this play is to be about, will have to be answered by the director . . . if you can find her."

The organization's cadre of management carries the primary responsibility for communicating the VOC. Readers of books on organizational change have probably been dosed with the idea that the chief executive of the company is the primary communicator of the organization's VOC. Nothing could be further from the truth! The primary communicator of the change vision is the cadre of management. Each member of that cadre takes primary responsibility for communicating the vision to his department, section, or branch (i.e., his direct reports). Yes, of course, the chief executive must communicate the vision to the cadre of management, but there are only a few managers compared with the number of workers. Only the cadre can effectively carry the VOC to the workers.

Let's validate this communication idea with some common sense. Imagine an organization that has 2,000 employees scattered across the globe. Imagine how difficult it would be for that company to complete an organizational change on target, on time, and on budget with the chief executive as the primary communicator of change. While the folks that work in the same building as the chief executive might hear about the future from his lips, the vast majority of the workforce is not likely to see or hear him for more than a few minutes per year (even on video or the intranet). In addition, the vast majority of the work force already has someone to look to for information and direction about the company. The person to look to is the nearest boss or manager—the division, department, branch, or section head.

Members of the cadre of management must also work through, develop, and communicate their own unit's VOC that fits with the VOC for the entire organization. They, in fact, need to develop a picture of how the organization's vision would look in their unit. Some managers develop their unit's vision while others do a participative form of vision development with some, or all, of the workers in the unit. While it would be difficult to describe the best way to do this, managers who use the participative method clearly have an easier time communicating their unit's vision because they have a head start on the communication with their workers.

Direction of Workers

 MIND-CLEARING EXAMPLE

Imagine the key assistants to a director observing members of the theater company preparing for the new play. Imagine that those preparations are clearly off target and not aligned with what the assistants know to be the director's intentions. Imagine those assistants doing nothing about it! When asked by company members for their input, imagine the assistants shrugging and saying, "Just do what you want to do."

The direction of the workers is clearly the most important part of the change mission of the cadre of management. While the chief executive acts as director for the cadre of management, the primary job of direction in the organization falls to the cadre of management. It is up to each manager to provide the direction needed by her workers to be able to play their new roles after the organizational change.

This critical leadership job for the cadre of management might best be described with the word *direction,* used in its theatrical sense. Each manager has the responsibility to bring the play (the VOC) to life in her unit, and does it much like a theater director. And just as a theater director won't get far by ordering her company to a new play, a manager will not be able to bring about changes in the workers' behavior with orders!

The two primary tasks of each member of the cadre of management are to (1) get her workers under contract for the upcoming new work and the change work needed for the transition, and (2) to work closely with the workers (like a theater director) as the workers begin to alter their roles to fit the organization's and unit's VOC. While I will say much more about getting workers under contract in Chapter 7, suffice it to say that the cadre's job is to get employees to agree to alter their roles in the upcoming change and to do the necessary work to think through and prepare for those new roles.

Giving workers direction for new roles needs to be done as conscientiously, carefully, and respectfully as a theater director working with professional actors. In fact, managers could learn a great deal by following steps taken by theater directors:

- Doing their homework on the vision (the play).
- Having a plan for directing the workers.
- Concentrating on ensuring that the workers understand the vision and where they need to go.
- Acting as coaches to the professional workers (actors) as they work through how they will play their roles in the new work.
- Coaching through a variety of means to meet the workers' needs for communication style: explanation, example, demonstration, and rehearsal.
- Keeping in mind that the director's job is to get the vision into place through the actions of the actors.

During direction toward new roles, mangers should be as cautious as theater directors not to invade the domain of the workers, acting respectfully and in appreciation of the workers' talents. And yet, proceeding steadily toward readying those workers for the new performance that is sure to come as the organization shifts to its new work.

In this description of change leadership from the cadre of managers, I am being very careful to recommend a theater director's style of respect and persuasion, accompanied with the director's commitment and certainty of movement to a new play. I would not want you to interpret my recommended leadership approach as overly soft or hard. I want you to hear a common sense approach from the cadre of managers that says, "Come, let us change this organization to be what it needs to be and we are here to help you make the changes in your roles that only you can make. Let us work together for success!"

Developing Personal Management Roles

MIND-CLEARING EXAMPLE

Imagine the key assistants to a director listening politely to her announcement of the decision for a new play. Then imagine those key assistants taking no initiative to think through what their personal roles will need to be in the new production or in its preparation. Imagine one assistant saying to another, "I hear what the boss expects about the new production, but I am really comfortable with what I have been doing on the old play, so I think I will stick with that!"

The responsibility of the cadre of managers during change is to both direct the workers toward their new roles and develop their own new roles. We cannot expect change from a workforce that does not see its managers changing their roles right before the workers' eyes! Each manager must adjust her own role in day-to-day work, under the direction of her manager, demonstrating initiative in role development and adding energy and enthusiasm to the workers.

Some or all of the following behaviors will need to change for each manager involved in the organizational change:

- How she describes the organization's and her unit's future to customers and employees.
- The goals for her unit in the organization.
- The way she approaches or solves the unit's business problems.
- Who she spends her time with in the organization.
- Which customers she visits and what she talks about with them.
- The kinds of internal projects she visits and watches.
- Her day-to-day language and vocabulary.

The bottom line is this: if the ways managers spend their time do not change, then the organization is not likely to change. And if the workers do not see the cadre of management working on new ways of operating after the change, workers are unlikely to take the change in their roles seriously even if managers show up to coach and direct.

THE CHANGE MISSION
OF THE WORKERS:
DEVELOPING ROLES

 MIND-CLEARING EXAMPLE

Imagine actors and stage hands in a theater company sitting on their hands while the director and his key assistants do the transition work for a new play. Imagine actors who have been assigned roles in a new play taking no initiative to learn their lines or work out their own ideas for portraying their roles. Imagine a seasoned actor saying, "Ok, Mr. Director, just tell me exactly how you want me to act this part and I'll follow your instructions to the letter."

Workers in organizations are just as responsible for initiating change as managers. Workers must take the initiative in order for most of the organization's change work to get done. The workers' jobs are as the change implementers for the company. The workers' primary change mission is to

- assimilate the description of the desired future for the organization so they can enact it during their day-to-day work,
- work under the direction of the cadre of management to complete and refine alteration to work processes and PET, and
- work under the direction of the cadre of management to develop their own altered work roles as they will need to be played in the VOC.

Assimilation of the Vision of
Organizational Change

 MIND-CLEARING EXAMPLE

Imagine the professional actors in a theater company not studying the script for the new play. Imagine them dozing as the director talks through her ideas for the play. Imagine actors saying something like, "Gee, this play is so different from the last one we performed that I can't really relate to it."

Workers are responsible for assimilating both the VOC and the vision for their specific unit. Assimilation means to hear, digest, understand, put in context, and interpret the job implications. This statement of worker responsibility for change might stretch the imagination of folks in some organizations, but imagine professional actors in a play not being expected to understand the play. Of course the workers must have an understanding of the organization and unit vision, just like sports players must understand the game as well as their individual roles.

Not all workers will assimilate a new direction in the same way or at the same rate. Some workers will be able to think their way through the vision, others will need a thorough explanation from a manager or from other workers. Some will even need to see pieces of the vision in action (either in their organization or in another) before they can get the essential idea of the vision. Regardless of the process or speed of assimilation, two points stand out: (1) there is no substitute for the workers' knowledge of the VOC, and (2) there is no ducking personal responsibility for assimilation. It is a key part of the job in today's world of work. Workers must actively cooperate with their manager as she does her duty and communicates both the organizational and unit visions.

Altering Work PET

MIND-CLEARING EXAMPLE

Imagine the professional actors in a theater company staying uninvolved in the preparations for the new play. Imagine them unwilling to walk through their parts in rehearsal as the director tries to see the play in motion. Imagine these actors not cooperating with the costume and make-up designers to work out the look of their characters in the play.

While managers will most likely lead the efforts to alter work processes and PET, it is the workers who will inevitably be the arms and legs of those alterations. Whether it be working on small ad hoc teams, the total unit team, or individually, the workers will do a majority of the many tasks to be done in transitioning the organization from old work to new work. Such transition work may be anything from the design and mapping of new work processes to the writing of new work procedures. The work may be anything from assisting in the selection of new equipment to the installation/testing of that equipment and writing of the equipment operating guidelines.

Outside vendors or consultants may be hired by the organization to assist in process and/or PET alteration, but sooner or later, the organization's workers will be expected to take over those processes and the PET. Taking over can mean anything from breaking in tools to refining procedures and guidelines or rewriting those guidelines in light of how the new work actually comes together. Just as the actors and stagehands must finally work out the details of the performance, so do workers refine the details of work processes and equipment, and they must do it with initiative and energy.

Developing Personal Work Roles

MIND-CLEARING EXAMPLE

Imagine the professional actors in a theater company not working to understand and develop their assigned characters. Imagine them waiting like wooden Indians as the director spells out every last move, gesture, posture, and verbal inflection. Imagine professional actors not taking responsibility for ensuring that their portrayal fits into the overall production!

Developing personal work roles for new work is the most important change mission of the workers. Organizations literally don't change an iota until the workers do things differently in their roles. Workers, with the directions of their manager, must develop the day-to-day way of behaving that uses altered tools in altered processes to do the new work of the organization. The role development process is similar to what an actor goes through as she works out the details of how she will behave on the stage: what she will say, how she will move, what inflection she will use, and so on. The worker must count on feedback from her manager just like the actor counts on feedback from the director. The professional worker knows that she cannot see herself at work any more that the actor can see herself on stage.

The workers' change responsibility is not to depend on detailed orders and instructions from the manager but to take responsibility in working through the details of their altered roles themselves. In working through the details of the roles, workers will find the needed shortcuts and efficiencies that a manager could never identify and recommend.

We have had managers and workers alike say that it was not the job of the worker to develop the new roles. "And, besides," many of them said, "the average worker couldn't do that anyway." We know that such ideas are out there, but we have seen workers time and again do a beautiful job of developing new roles even with a minimum of direction, provided they knew the big picture of what needed to be accomplished at both the organization and unit levels.

We have found that workers will develop their roles in very different ways and at different rates, much like the vision assimilation process.

It is the manager's job to honor and respect the workers' style and needs as they go through the process of thinking and trying how they will need to act in their new work.

TEAMWORK IN ORGANIZATIONAL CHANGE

 MIND-CLEARING EXAMPLE

Imagine actors rehearsing a play by themselves rather than with the rest of the cast. Imagine the costume designers not working with set designers and lighting specialists to pick out colors for fabrics. Imagine the director not working with the stage manager and the lighting manager to come to agreement on the look and feel of the set for each act.

Teamwork is critical for organizational change—on target, on time, and on budget. Just as the organization works together as a team while doing old work, they will need to be a team when the transition is made to new work. And teamwork will be required during the completion of the change work necessary for the transition.

While the chief executive leads the management change team, each manager leads his unit's change team in order to ensure that all the transition work is done. In addition, as I will discuss in detail in Chapter 9, the manager must lead his organization to continue to accomplish the unit's old work while the change work is going on.

But just as the director of the play has the primary responsibility for bringing the play to life on the stage, it is the chief executive who has the greatest responsibility for the organization's change teamwork. She and she alone can bring the passion, energy, and enthusiasm that will be needed to ensure that all of the organization's employees—its change leaders—will catch the change spirit, assume their change leadership roles, and go forward as a team to complete the change on target, on time, and on budget.

PART FOUR

Engineering Change

Engineering organizational change is all about altering the four critical categories of stuff that make up the organization—its vision, its work process(es), PET, and performance management systems. Implementation planning is first and foremost a case of deciding exactly and precisely what alterations will be required in each of the components. (Of course, a single component has many pieces that may need to be impacted for the change to occur. For example, rarely does an organizational change require alteration of a single work process or a single piece of equipment.) Then one must decide how the required alterations are to be made. The physical change piece is all about making the required alterations and ensuring that they are done and done right.

Knowing where we are in an engineering change is a matter of auditing the status of required alterations and dealing with the reality of what we find:

- Either processes have been altered or they have not. New procedures to allow people to follow those processes have been written and distributed or they have not. The old processes and their supporting procedures have been dismantled/destroyed or they have not.
- Either the new PET is on board and working or it is not. Either the guidelines for operating the new PET have been written and distributed or they have not. Either the old PET and its operating instructions have been removed and/or disabled or they have not.
- Either the performance contract for each and every manager and employee impacted by the change has been altered and negotiated with them or it has not. Either each and every manager and employee has been trained on the new processes and new PET or they have not. And so on!

4

Engineering and Communicating Vision

 MIND-CLEARING EXAMPLE

Imagine a director who selects the new play but who fails to communicate it to the theater company. Or imagine the company receiving its only information about a new play from backstage gossip. Imagine the company receiving only a half-page set of bullet points instead of a completed script.

CONSTRUCT THE DETAILED VISION FOR ORGANIZATIONAL CHANGE

The first requirement of engineering organizational change is to construct and fully communicate a clear, detailed vision of the desired organizational future. The VOC is the picture of the future that is painted by the leader. Not any picture of the future will be good enough. It must be a picture that has the right stuff! If the employees of an organization are going to be asked to change, they need to know what that change will look like. And they need as much information about that change as they can get so that they can integrate that picture of the future into their current way of thinking.

Just as a theater company needs a script to understand the new play it is to perform, organization members need a vision to understand what the leader wants the company to be in the future. And therein lies the rub. Leaders have traditionally understated their visions of the future, relying on five or six bullet points on a single page to communicate what they want their companies to become. The simple truth of the matter is that such a vision statement is totally unsatisfactory as a tool for organizational change.

For a vision to be useful, it must be thought through and detailed much more like the script for a play than like the bullet points we see on presentation slides. To make the point:

> Imagine a director who introduces his theater company to the upcoming performance with the following description instead of a script. "We will be conducting a new play that people are going to rave about. It will be a musical comedy, set in contemporary New York, with songs sung by heavily costumed cats and great choreography! Doesn't this sound exciting?" Imagine the company asking for more details and being told, "It's all right there," and the director repeating the description just given.

A VOC must be constructed so that it captures the real spirit of the desired change and be engineered

- to show organization members
- performing work processes and
- using the PET required by those work processes.

There are three simple steps for constructing a VOC. The steps are (1) to design the direction of change, (2) to detail the VOC, and (3) to test the vision with a cross section of the organization that will be implementing the change.

Design the Direction of the Desired Change

It is the role of the leader to ensure that there is a clear direction for any desired organizational change. Over the years, we have seen successful changes that have started with a design that came from everything from an autocratic decree to a heavily participative process involving hundreds of people in the organization and its marketplace. Our favorite approach, and the one we think works best, uses a mixture of participation from those organization members who can see the future and decisive leadership that is willing to cut off debate at some point and make a call. "Making a call" means stating for the record the direction of the desired change. An example of the desired direction of change is Bell Helicopter's vision of "having the world's most reliable helicopters and the world's most responsive service to its customers."

Detail the Vision for Organizational Change

It is one thing to have the direction of organizational change in mind; it is another to give that direction a voice or a presence that organization members can grasp. In the detailing step, we want to paint a richly textured picture of how the organization will operate after the desired change.

Some of the best visions we have seen for organizational change are considerably longer and more detailed than a few short bullet points on a half sheet of paper. One of our long-time clients was a COO of a large financial organization. He made one pass at articulating his vision for the year 2000 for the firm's distribution system made of some 4,000 offices. His first pass was made using the traditional approach of six quick bullet points on one page. He and his direct reports conducted a half-day session with the next 20 managers to explain the vision using the six bullet points as the primary explanation tool. As the sessions were going along, the COO leaned over to me and said, "I can tell that our message is not getting across. What do we do?"

The COO finished that session and went back to the drawing board, or in his case, the PC. Over the next week, he turned the bullet point vision into a 20-plus-page short story that illustrated in great detail the bullet points. The story was about a prospective customer who tried to do business with the financial organization in the year 2000. He detailed what a prospective customer did, how the organization responded, and how actual people in the organization worked with the customer—what they said and exactly what they did. After the short story was complete, the COO gave it to the same 20 managers who had been in the first explanation session. Their response was simple and straightforward: "Now we get it. Now we understand what the bullet points mean! And we like it!"

A good way to get the VOC detailed is to simply put a vision team in a room and ask them to write on wall charts answers to the following sets of questions:

- *Organization Members.* Who will be working or behaving in new ways after the desired change is put into effect? How will they be acting that is different than the way they act today? What will be the accepted way we do things around here? Where will they be located in the organization? Who will they be relating to or working with that is different than today? How will that interaction look?
- *Work Processes.* What work processes or steps for getting work done will be different than the steps that are being used now? What parts of the organization will be doing things differently after the change?
- *PET.* What tools will people be using in work processes? In what buildings and in what locations will they be in? What kind of computer will they have? What software will the people be using in different parts of the organization? What will this software be doing for them? What will they be doing "on the screen" vs. "off the screen?"

Once the vision team has sketched answers to the questions, the team (or an appointed small drafting committee) can combine the team's answers into a form that will make sense for the situation— either a short story format or a detailed bullet point slide presentation.

Test the Vision for Organizational Change

We don't know if we have a vision that will work for organizational change unless we test it with the members of the organization. We want the vision message tested with representatives of the organization to ensure that it is understandable, and that it passes the tests I talked about earlier. We want to ensure in the testing process that organization members see the vision as valid, complete, possible, resourceable, and compelling.

We think a good way to do the test of the VOC is to get a cross-sectional group of a dozen employees together in a briefing room and ask them to answer the following questions (putting the folks into three teams of four helps the responses):

- What did you hear as the vision for this organization's future?

- Can you see how this vision will work to win with customers, investors, and employees?
- What parts of the vision need more detail for the sake of clarity?
- Can you see the organization being successful in implementing this vision?
- Do you think the organization can get the resources it needs to achieve this vision?
- What about the vision will be attractive, engaging, and challenging to the organization and its workers?
- Is this a vision that you could explain to others in the organization? What parts of the vision would be tough to explain?

When you look at the responses to questions like these, you will know whether you have stated your vision in a way the organization can understand. If answers from the test employees show that they understand the vision and find it doable and compelling, you may have a vision that will serve you well in the change process. If not, clarify or add more detail to your vision. Whatever you do, don't start change without a clear and understandable vision of the future.

One of our clients recently finished such a test with his organization. The president of this international company and some 20 members of his organization had just completed the design and detailing of their vision for the future. They wanted to gauge employee reaction to the vision before they went into organization-wide communication. About 20 employees representing both the headquarters and the field organizations were brought together for a two-hour session in which the president and his management team walked the group through the vision of the future. The president and his team found out that their vision and direction for the future were clear and compelling; but they also found out that the growth objectives in the vision were too numerous and overwhelming. Is that all, you say? Yep, it's that simple. The unfortunate fact of the matter is that many organizations launch a full-scale change effort without a simple vision test like the one used by our client!

CONSTRUCT THE PARTNER TO THE VISION: THE CASE FOR CHANGE

 MIND-CLEARING EXAMPLE

Imagine a director who hands out the script for a new play without saying anything about the current play that the theater company is performing nightly. When asked about the status of the current play, imagine the director saying, "Oh, I don't know what we're going to do with it. Just start thinking about this new script."

Organization members seem to respond better to organizational change when they understand why the change is necessary and/or desirable. The case for organization change is, therefore, a rational explanation of the need to change put in terms of value to organization members. There are several stakeholders (persons or entities that have something "at stake" with the organization) involved with every organizations. But one stakeholder is more critical than others for the change. An organizational change must be made by the organization's members, and they are the ones who need to see both the wisdom and the personal consequences of the change if they are to be vitally involved in making that change happen.

The case for change is derived from another kind of future vision for the organization—the future the organization and its employees will face if changes are *not made* in the way it is doing business. The method for deriving the case for change comes from a simple visioning process that predicts the organization's vitality and health level if it continues to operate into the future in just the way it does now.

Develop the Case for Change

It is the role of the leader to ensure that there is a clear and compelling case for any desired organizational change. For the purposes of engineering organizational change, the method the leader uses to identify the case for change is largely immaterial. But if the case for change is not strong, change will be very unlikely to happen as the leader wants it to. Any attempt to change an organization is a big undertaking, an undertaking that always has real risks to the continued healthy operation of the organization, to uninterrupted service to customers, to the earnings of the investors, and to the total working compensation of the employees.

The case for change drives simple bottom line statements for the organization's three stakeholders. The bottom line for the case for change from the customer point of view is simple: the case must describe a situation that the customer will find undesirable to keeping up the business relationship with the organization. The bottom line for the case for change from the investor point of view is simple: the case must describe a situation that investors will see as undesirable for themselves at a personal level. The bottom line for the case for change from the employee point of view is simple: the case must describe a situation that organization members will see as undesirable for themselves at a personal level. If a compelling case for change cannot be honestly and realistically made, the organization would be better off without it!

Detail the Case for Organizational Change

A good way to get the case for change detailed is to simply put the same vision team in a room and ask them to write on wall charts answers to the following set of questions:

- *Customers.* If our organization does not change, will our customers be more or less inclined to do business with us? How will our relationship look with customers in *x* years? How will our way of working with customers be compared to the way our strongest competitors relate to customers?
- *Investors.* If our organization does not change, will our investors be more or less inclined to keep their investment with us? How will they see us as a stock recommendation—buy, hold, or sell?
- *Organization Members.* If our organization does not change, will our employees be more or less secure in our business? How stable will employment be with our firm? What about development and training opportunities?

Once the vision team has sketched answers to the above questions, the team (or a small appointed drafting committee) can combine the team's answers into a detailed presentation. This presentation must emphasize whatever facts are available to best make the case and to create a sense of urgency for the change.

Test the Case for Organizational Change

' We don't know if we have a case for change that will work unless we test it with the members of the organization. We want to see if people can identify with personal consequences for themselves as we unfold the case for change.

We think a good way to do the test of the case for change is to get a cross-sectional group of a dozen employees together in a briefing room and ask them to answer the following questions (putting the folks into three teams of four helps the responses):

- What did you hear as the case for change?
- How plausible is that case to you?
- What do you see as the ramifications of not changing our organization's current way of doing business for customers, investors, and employees?
- Do you think it is important for the organization to change, given the potential ramifications to customers, investors, and employees?
- Do you think it is important to begin that change now? Why or why not?
- What do you see as the possible consequences to you and your job if the organization continues its current way of doing business?
- What could happen to you and your job if the organization is not successful in changing the way it does business?

When you look at the responses to questions like these, you will know whether you have stated your case for change in a way the organization can incorporate. If answers from the test employees show undesirable personal consequences, you may have a case that will serve you well in the change process. If not, remake your case or abandon your plans to make a change!

ENSURE MANAGEMENT UNDERSTANDING AND EXPECTATION

 MIND-CLEARING EXAMPLE

Imagine a director who is communicating the new play to the bit actors and stagehands while the lead actors and the stage manager look on and shake their heads in disagreement with everything the director says. Imagine the musicians hearing the director with one ear while hearing the conductor mumble to those around him, "Really dumb idea."

Organization members react to their bosses. Period. If you want to make an organizational change, you better have all the managers in the organization signed up and ready to play or the change is not likely to work. It is critical for all managers of the cadre of management to

- understand the vision and case for organizational change,
- understand your expectation that they be a part of leading/managing the change, and
- be totally committed to making the change happen.

Many leaders would think this is a tall order, and it may be in some organizations. But our advice is simple, do not attempt a change without the managers on board. If the change is required for business success, you can either get all your managers on board or change to managers who will be on board.

We have seen more change efforts scuttled by uncommitted managers than by any other problem. Managers who are not committed to the change present a clear mixed signal to employees. If top management signals a change but other managers don't go along with it, the employees are in a box and they will usually resolve their mixed feelings by taking the position of the manager who is closest to them on the organization chart. All organization members are responsible to somebody in the organizational hierarchy. That's what we figure out after only a few days on the job. It is totally nonsensical to ask an organization member to put her job in jeopardy by taking up a change that her boss doesn't agree with.

It has always struck us as very interesting that organizations go through tough exercises to face the reality of their marketplace and decide that they *must* change and then serve up that change to the organization as though the change were *optional!* We don't mean that managers stand in front of employees and use the word *optional* with regard to change; they don't. But they do talk about the change in such "iffy" and participative tones that employees wind up feeling the change is optional. Sometimes managers go out of their way to be sensitive to employee feelings, and ask employees about the change rather than announcing that the change will occur.

If the organization needs to change for prosperity's or survival's sake, then the change is not optional! Announce the change. Don't ask the organization what it wants to do. If the change is required for organizational prosperity or survival reasons, there is no way out. The organization must change. Organization members always have the option of going along with the change or not—or in other words, staying in the organization and cooperating in the change or leaving the organization.

When we receive harsh criticism about our "change is not an option" message, we ask, "Should the director of a new play allow key players to stay in the cast and act a different play on stage while the rest of the company acts the new performance?"

Conducting Management Work-through Sessions

We have found that getting management on board for a change is much easier if what we call *work-through sessions* are conducted with all managers who have a part or stake in the change. The two purposes of the sessions are to allow managers (1) to absorb the idea of the change and the resulting organization structure, and (2) to work through the ramifications of the change for themselves and their troops. The sessions also provide the opportunity to get management "in the know" before their employees get pulled into the change. Managers must be in the know first, lest their authority and credibility be undercut with their employees who need to know and feel that their boss is part of the leadership structure of the company.

Management work-through sessions are simply meetings of groups of mangers with the leaders of the company to discuss an impending change. The key idea is to allow the managers the opportunity to hear about the impending change firsthand, to ask questions about the change, and even to challenge the change—both from a rational and technical point of view. After all, we pay managers to question and challenge ideas to ensure their validity before action. So why not allow that challenge here? In many such sessions, we have seen great ideas developed that add to the design of the vision and the case for change.

We have also seen the effect of different learning styles in such discussions. With certain adult learners, the need to question and criticize something—to state "that will never work" and so forth—is necessary for hearing and understanding. The leader's role is to keep his cool during the discussions and trust that most managers will both understand the impending change and recognize that their jobs are to make that change happen.

Now before we get into the detailed methods for a work-through session, let's remember where we are in engineering organizational change. We have already developed and tested our vision for organizational change and the case for change. Several of the managers we are about to address may have already been involved in developing either the vision or the case for change. In either case, the change has been decided and there is no turning back. Given these stated conditions, we have found the following ten steps to be useful in work-through sessions:

1. The organization's leader(s) start the meeting with an introduction that explains the purpose of the session.
   - "Our purpose today is to talk through an organizational change that we will be making to ensure the prosperity/survival of our company."
   - "My expectation is that you will involve yourself in the session to fully understand the change that all of us, the company's management team, will be responsible for implementing."
2. The leader follows with a description of the impending change (i.e, VOC, including the organizational structure) and the rationale for the change.
3. The leader breaks the audience of managers into small teams of four or five to discuss and report on the following questions:
   - What did you hear as the most important part of the VOC?
   - What did you hear as the most important business reason for the organizational change?
   - What are the advantages of the impending change to the company?
   - What are the disadvantages of the impending change?

- What are the biggest obstacles to fully implementing the change?
- What are your ideas about the best ways to go about the implementation of such a change?

4. The leader moves from team to team, making herself available for questions and clarifications as the teams work through the questions.

5. The leader calls for the teams to present their answers to the questions and arranges for those answers to be recorded for later use.
   - The leader's goal during this step is to hear the audience working through the understanding and assimilation of the information about the impending change.
   - The leader's challenge will be to hear these answers as part of a communication process and not as direct criticism of the leader's choice of a direction for impending change.

6. The leader now shifts emphasis and asks each individual manager to consider the following questions for his/her organization (unit, department, section, etc.):
   - What will be the ramifications of the change for your organization?
   - In presenting the impending change to your organization, what will be the most critical part of the case for change?

7. The leader might ask for volunteers (three or four managers) to share their answers with the audience.

8. The leader wraps up the discussion by asking the audience of managers to respond as one large team—because that is what they are—to the following questions:
   - On a one-to-seven scale, how clear are we on the general direction of the impending change?
   - On a one-to-seven scale, how clear are we on the case for the change?

9. The leader records the number of responses in each category, one to seven (with seven meaning "very clear") and responds to the results. A normal audience that hears and understands an impending change will have a normal distribution of scores between five and six points on the seven-point scale. If there are scores in the three-to-four range, the leader can ask the general audience (without identifying the managers whose scores were low) how she can further clarify the vision and case for organizational change.

10. The leader closes the session with the following announcements:
    - "We will get back together again to discuss and finalize our action plans for implementing the impending change."
    - "Before that meeting, I (or your boss) will visit with each of you one-on-one to ensure we are in sync about the change."

During the conduct of the work-through sessions, it is critical for the leader to lead the change in word and deed. We mean the following:

- The leader should have a presence and tone that says, "We are making this change happen because it is our job. I am in control of the change, and it will happen on time, on target, and on budget." The leader, like an actor, must look serious and committed to the change.
- The leader should clearly convey that the change is not optional.
- The leader should clearly convey her expectation that all the mangers in the firm will be on board and help with the implementation of the change.
- The leader should convey her excitement about the opportunity to change the organization for the better and her confidence that the change will be good for the organization.
- The leader should convey the message that the change will be done in an orderly planned way with each member of the management team doing his or her part to make the change happen.

We cannot overemphasize the importance of leadership presence during this critical step in engineering change. These manager work-through sessions are critical for the organizational change and the leader must look and be serious and committed or the sessions will move the change *back* and not forward!

Testing Management to Ensure They Are on Board

Management work-through is not complete until we have ensured that all of our managers are on board with the change. The only way to ensure understanding of the impending change and willingness to be a part of leading the organization through it is to conduct a face-to-face meeting, one-on-one with each manager in the organization. In that meeting the leader hears and sees for herself that the managers do understand both the vision and the case for change. The leader might ask questions such as:

- What do you think the most important part of the change will be for your unit?
- How do you plan to explain the case for change to your team?

The bottom line is that the questions are not important. What is important is that the leader interacts enough with each manager about the change to reassure herself that they understand the vision and case for change.

After ensuring understanding, the leader must move on to reassure herself that each manager is willing to support the change. (Remember that we said the change is not optional for the organization. That doesn't mean that all organization members will be willing to go along with it.) The best way to deal with the "readiness to support" issue is simply to ask the managers point blank if they are ready to support the leader in making the change happen on target, on time, and on budget. Because many managers would be reluctant to give any answer other than *yes,* the leader should hold out an honest offer to allow them to consider the questions and come see the leader before the week is over. The leader might say, "If I have not heard from you to the contrary by the end of business this week, I will assume you are on board."

Now get this, the leader closes the one-on-one meetings with the managers with our cultural signal of business agreement—the handshake. This handshake clearly symbolizes a business agreement and is the single most compelling action the leader can take with a manager. The handshake means that the manager understands the impending change and the leader's expectation that the manager will be involved in implementing it.

For organizations with more than one level of management between the leader and the employees, management work-through sessions will need to be conducted a layer of management at a time until the entire chain of command has been brought to a common level of understanding and willingness to implement. That is, we do not want to put several layers of management in the same room at the same time for work-through sessions for a key reason. We want to maintain the authority of the chain of command and the credibility of each manager by having her work through the change message before her direct reports. We want her to feel free to question and even argue about the upcoming change and get on board with it before she works the change with her direct reports. If a manager and her direct reports hear about a change at the same time, the direct reports will wonder why their boss wasn't in on or privy to the leadership decision about change.

COMMUNICATE THE VISION THE RIGHT WAY

 MIND-CLEARING EXAMPLE

Imagine a director who is trying to communicate the new play to a theater company with an opener like, "OK folks, I'm only going to tell you the contents of this play one time." Or imagine that director giving out only one copy of the script for the entire theater company. Better yet, imagine the director who says, "I don't want to bore you with all the details of the script, so here is a letter summarizing the key parts."

Communicating the vision and case for organization change the right way is a simple idea that is tough to execute. The *right way* means to communicate the message so that every member of the organization that is changing gets to hear the message enough times and in enough ways to be able to understand what they need to do. Our experience is that most leaders start the communication process with good intentions, but they typically do not follow through with the detailed steps that are needed. Engineering change depends on a systematic approach to communicating change.

Plan for Communicating Change

Communicating a new play to a theater company of two dozen can be a relatively simple exercise of calling one all-hands meeting and talking everyone through the change. But for an organization of 14,000 employees spread over 30 countries, communication is not quite so easy. For a change situation like this, a comprehensive communication plan is needed. The plan must identify the specific populations among the employees, the specific locations of those employees, their work shifts/schedules, the languages and/or cultures involved, the communication devices that are available, and the overall timetable for impending change. The bottom line requirement for the communication plan is that it be an engineering solution to the problem of getting each person the information he needs, when he needs it, to have him be involved in a change that occurs on target, on time, and on budget.

Use All Available Communication Devices

Most companies already have a variety of communication devices that they use in their day-to-day businesses. The primary decision communication device in an organization is the chain of command—the direct linkages between a boss and every member of the organization. This primary channel must be used to communicate about organizational change or the members of the organization will not see information about impending change as having anything important to do with them. Other communication devices, like electronic bulletin boards, newsletters, training classes, safety meetings, and staff meetings are already standard and accepted means of communication. These other devices should be used to accompany and/or reinforce the chain of command message, but they can never substitute for it!

We know that it is not popular in some circles to even mention a phrase from the past like *chain of command,* but the truth is, every organization has one, and the employees in every organization respond to it. This chain of command linkage between boss and organization member is a primary mechanical connection that makes up a part of the structure of any organization. Organizations cannot be changed on target, on time, and on budget without using the chain of command linkage. Imagine a theater company without a director trying to get a new play ready and onto the stage.

Use Critical Communication Principles

There are four principles that we believe are required for effective communication about impending organizational change.

1. *Two-way communication.* This allows organization members to ask questions and give feedback about the change and is required for a high-comprehension level. We all need to interact in the communication process if we are to really get a message that is being communicated.
2. *Communication bases.* These should be considered when planning and executing communication. In short, some adults under-

stand new messages better if they see them in black and white; others understand better if they hear them; others need to experience the message by handling physical models or imagining themselves in the described situation. Because organizations are made up of all three communication types, leaders must ensure that their communication plan provides devices that cover all three bases.

3. *Repetition.* This is required for any of us to get organization messages. While the number of repetitions recommended ranges from three or four all the way to seven or more, our position is simple. Plan to communicate to every single person in the organization significantly more times than once to ensure the message about impending change is delivered.

4. *Rich, face-to-face communication.* This is required for organization members to communicate at maximum levels of effectiveness on critically important subjects. Messages about impending organizational change must be delivered face-to-face or organization members will not have their communication needs at all met. Put the details in a follow-up letter that comes later, but put the essential messages about impending change in play in a face-to-face environment. Face-to-face communication can be a real problem in today's world of companies that are dispersed over the country or the globe. Employees in dispersed locations have to hear about change in face-to-face meetings with their local bosses. And the local bosses need to hear it first from their bosses back at headquarters. That usually means travel, there is no way around it.

Agree to and Use
Communication Standards

All managers involved in the communication of change must be in sync with how they are going to communicate to the organization. We have found it useful to get the managers to agree on the following four standards for communication that provide basic guidelines for the communication process.

1. Communication of the change will be done from a comprehensive, coordinated plan.
2. All change messages will be developed and delivered ensuring that

- there is a redundancy of message delivery (i.e., each employee receives the message multiple times), and
- the message will be delivered through a variety of channels (verbal, written, face-to-face meetings, newsletters, and training programs).

3. All messages will be tested for understandability before delivery.
4. We will ensure that our management actions match the words in our message.

Imagine how well communication might work in an organization if all its managers agreed to and used such communication standards. One of the primary responsibilities of any manager is to communicate important messages about the running of the organization. When managers begin to take such responsibility seriously, organizational change will get much easier than it is today in many organizations that treat communication as "just more of that soft stuff."

Work Your Communication Plan to Desired Results

Plan your work and work your plan. In the context of communicating change, working your plan is important, and working your plan well, crisply, and in a well-organized way can take you a long way toward successful organizational change. We have seen great damage done to change efforts by managers who are unprepared to communicate change. We can hardly expect an organization to change on target, on time, and on budget if the organization's managers cannot even communicate about the impending change on target, on time, and on budget! Imagine what it says to an organization when its managers start the change communication meeting late without needed materials, and with unfocused projectors, poorly prepared slides, and unrehearsed remarks!

Leaders have not mastered change until they can communicate about organizational change with the same effectiveness and efficiency in which they communicate routine changes in production runs, part numbers, and sales prices.

ENSURE EMPLOYEE TRANSLATION OF THE VISION

 MIND-CLEARING EXAMPLE

Imagine a director who is handing out scripts for the new play. When an actor asks, who am I in the new play, the director simply responds, "Oh, I don't know. Just read the whole thing, and we'll work all that out later." Or worse yet, imagine the director saying, "I haven't even thought about you in the context of the new play. But just give it a read anyway."

Organization members are not ready to begin an organizational change until they can personally relate to it. The purpose of personal application sessions is to bring all employees affected by the impending change to a level of comprehension and to ensure that they are on board for the change. Personal application sessions are very similar to the manager work-through sessions I described earlier.

Every manager whose department or unit is affected by the change must conduct personal application sessions with her workers. The process includes a meeting of all employees reporting to that manager followed by a face-to-face, one-on-one session between manager and each employee. We have found the following nine steps useful for the sessions between the manager and her team of employees.

1. The manager starts the meeting with an introduction that explains the purpose of the session.
   - "Our purpose today is to talk through an organizational change that we will be making to ensure the prosperity/survival of our company."
   - "The goal of this session is to help you understand the impending change, what it will mean to you and your job, and to get your initial sign-up for the change."
2. The manager follows with a description of the impending change (the VOC and the case for the change).

3. The manager breaks the audience of employees into small teams of three or four to discuss and report on the following questions:
   - What did you hear as the most important part of the VOC?
   - What did you hear as the most important business reason for the organizational change?
   - What do you see as the changes we will need to make in our jobs in this department?
   - What are your ideas about the best ways to implement these changes in our organization?

4. The manager walks among the groups making herself available for questions and clarifications as the teams work through the questions.

5. The manager calls for the teams to present their answers to the questions and arranges for those answers to be recorded for later use.

6. The manager now shifts emphasis and asks each individual to consider the following questions for his/her job:
   - What will be the ramifications of the change for your job?
   - What kinds of things will you need to change in your specific job?

7. The manager might ask for three or four volunteers to share their answers with the audience.

8. The manager wraps up the discussion by asking the employees to respond as one large team to the following questions:
   - On a one-to-seven scale, how clear are we on the general direction of the impending change?
   - On a one-to-seven scale, how clear are we on the case for the change?

   The manager records the number of responses in each category, one to seven (with seven meaning "very clear") and responds to the results. A normal audience that hears and understands an impending change will have a normal distribution of scores between four and six points on the seven-point scale. If there are scores in the two-to-three range, the leader can ask the general audience how she can further clarify the vision and case for organizational change.

9. The manager closes the session with the following announcements:
    - "We will get back together again to discuss and finalize our action plans for implementing the impending change."
    - "Before that meeting, I will visit with each of you one-on-one to ensure we are in sync about the change."

During the conduct of the personal application sessions, the manager must lead the change with the same serious and committed tone and attitude we identified earlier for the leaders of management workthrough sessions.

5
Engineering Processes and Procedures

MIND-CLEARING EXAMPLE

Imagine a director who assumes that everything that needs to be worked out about the actors' performances is in the script. Imagine not working out detailed gameplans for starting and stopping the music, when curtains are to open and close, when scenery and backdrops are to be changed, and when actors enter and leave the stage.

The second requirement of engineering organizational change is to alter and test all work processes and procedures needed for the organizational vision. Failing to alter work processes and still expecting change is akin to expecting the performance of a new play from a theater company that is still operating with the old script.

Implementation of a vision cannot occur until existing processes and procedures are physically altered/modified to accommodate the new direction. Implementation cannot occur until the machinery of the work flow is successfully altered and tested. In this chapter, we will focus on changing the physical steps the organization uses to get its work done to ensure that its vision of organizational change is achieved.

IDENTIFY THE PROCESS ALTERATIONS NEEDED FOR CHANGE

 MIND-CLEARING EXAMPLE

Imagine a director who has not worked through in her mind exactly what she wants the actors to do in their newly assigned roles. Imagine her knowing that she wants to depict young men in the streets committed to revolution, but has not yet visualized or communicated the manning of the barricades on stage. Or imagine the director who changes the company to a new play, but allows the actors to repeat the scenes from the old play!

If a theater company doesn't change what happens on stage, the audience will swear that the play has not changed despite the new name on the marquee. If the day-in and day-out steps organization members take as they go about their work do not change, then the organization has not changed despite any words, slogans, or banners to the contrary.

If you are inexperienced in the street-fighting of organizational change, you may be wondering why we are making such no-brainer assertions. After watching organizational change for 30 years, we will tell you that it is commonplace for organizations to come up with a statement of new direction or plan, a new VOC, and still conduct day-to-day operations in essentially the same way while leaving the optimists among the work force to wait for a miracle and the cynical to wait for the change effort to crater or be allowed to slowly fade away.

Change Requires Work Process Alterations

Our task in this chapter is to focus on the mechanical alteration of an organization's work processes in order to allow the organization to act out the VOC. By virtue of the mechanical nature of organizations, every organizational change requires at least one change in work process. Regardless of the kind of organizational change or the stimulus for organizational change, work process alterations will be required.

- If an organization decides to change its business strategy (i.e., to become the low-cost producer), many, if not all, of the organization's production processes will need to change to take out costly manufacturing steps or to alter the sequence of those steps. In addition, the company's marketing and sales processes would need to be altered to add selling steps and promotional materials that stress changed features of the organization's products. Moving to become the low-cost producer might also require different steps for determining initial product pricing as well as for negotiation.

- If an organization decides to change one of the tools that it uses in its business, process change will almost certainly be involved. Work steps will need to change in order to set up the new tool and in order to use the output of the new tool. A new software tool, for instance, will likely require new data elements to enter the software or new steps to use the output of the software.

- If an organization decides to make a change in its culture (i.e., "the way we do things around here"), several process changes will result as organization members begin to approach the job differently. For example, if the desired cultural change is to become more attentive to customers, changes will probably need to be made in the steps and mindsets used in customer service departments or help desks.

Start with an Inventory of Work Processes

The first step in identifying needed work process alterations is to systematically review the organization's work processes and visualize any alterations that will be needed, given the VOC. We have found it easier to identify work processes that will be affected by an impending change by looking through the organization's existing inventory of work processes. Figure 5.1 shows the work process inventory for a company in the oil and gas business. The detail of the process steps in Figure 5.1 are at about the right level for the exercise of identifying alterations needed to implement an organizational change.

In case the organization does not have a work process inventory—and many organizations do not—we have found the following list of generic processes to be a good starting point for discussion as organization members look for processes that will need to be altered.

**FIGURE 5.1 Exploration and Production Process Level 2 Detail—
Acquire, Divest Properties**

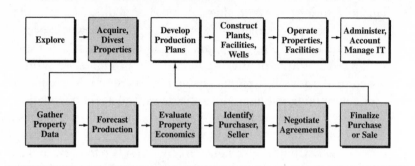

While the names organizations use for their own work processes vary greatly, almost all organizations need to use the following direct work processes in order to stay in business:

- Identify markets—groups of customers where the company's products and/or services might be sold.
- Develop products and/or services that can be sold in those markets.
- Get orders (make sales) for the company's products and/or services to individual customers within those markets.
- Produce and deliver the products and/or services that fulfill the customers' orders.
- Provide support to customers after delivery of products and/or services.
- Invoice customers for orders delivered and receive payments.

Obviously there are many subprocesses that make up each of these direct processes. For example, under the "get orders (make sales)" work process, companies frequently have subprocesses that identify prospects, research needs of those prospects, schedule sales calls, support sales calls, and conduct advertising campaigns.

In addition to the direct work processes cited above, organizations also have processes that manage the performance of

- the company as a whole,
- business processes cited above, and
- employees.

Firms also have processes that resource the other processes just described. Such resource processes have broad sweeping titles such as:

- Human resources
- Information technology
- Finance and administration
- Health, safety, and environment (HSE)
- Corporate communication and public relations
- Investor relations
- Legal services

Use a Team to Identify the Alterations Needed in Work Processes

We have found that one of the easier ways to identify work process impacts is to convene a team of employees that knows the organization very well. Have it go through either the company work process inventory or the generic inventory and look for connections between those processes and the VOC. The exercise that we use is a purely mechanical one. We give the team the following four instructions:

1. Spend 15 minutes getting as clear as you can on the VOC
2. Working from the actual or generic inventory list, answer the following questions for each work process in your organization:
   - Can we reach our VOC if the steps in this work process stay exactly like they are now?
   - If no, what steps must be altered to allow us to enact the VOC?
   - For each step that needs to be altered, what should be the desired result of that alteration?
3. Compile the results of your team's deliberations into the following categories:
   - Work processes that *do not* need alteration
   - Work processes that *do* need alteration
   - Steps in each work process that need alteration and the needed result of that alteration
4. Label your team's compiled results "Process Alterations Needed to Reach the VOC" and prepare to give team results during the action planning requirement.

There is nothing elegant about the process described above. This business of engineering change is a comprehensive mechanical exercise designed to be thorough, not elegant. While some organization members describe the process of identifying needed alterations as fun, others see it as pure drudgery. Regardless of your attitude, this step must be done. Many organizational changes have gone awry because the change planners did not take the time to comprehensively review all of their organization's processes and specifically identify the alteration work needed for the change.

ALTER AND TEST PROCESSES
CRITICAL TO THE CHANGE

 MIND-CLEARING EXAMPLE

Imagine a director who has an idea about what an actor in the new play should be doing, but who fails to work through the details with the actor. Or imagine the director working through the new ideas in his mind, but not actually testing them with the actor on stage. When asked specifically by an actor what he should do, the director responds, "Oh, don't worry, we will work that through on opening night."

The tendency in organizational change is to talk about what the organization needs to do but not really do it. That same tendency is alive and well in the area of work process alteration. The work process steps that have been identified for alteration must be physically altered. But where does this alteration take place? It takes place first and foremost on paper (or on a software program), and second when the organization's workers actually perform the new steps as a part of their day-to-day work.

Draw a Picture of the New Work Process

The key step in physically altering work processes is to draw a picture, much as an architect would do, of the new steps required for that work process. Most organizations today already have experience with process mapping and documentation. And many organizations are already using automated tools for such mapping—so use them! The purpose of this book is not to describe the well-developed field of process improvement or mapping. It is to make the point that many of the tools of process improvement, especially process mapping, apply in every organizational change!

We have had clients push back when we tell them that mapping process alterations is a must. Several have responded, "I thought we did all that during our emphasis on total quality management." Our response is simple. We must remap processes as a part of every organizational change or there will be no organizational change. Altering processes remains a requirement despite how detailed and tedious it might be. Imagine the theater director who makes the following bizarre statement, "No need to think through the details of roles in the new play, we did that detailed thinking for the old play."

Use a Team to Map and Test Work Processes

We have found that a team of knowledgeable employees can map work processes to show needed alterations quite easily. After forming the alteration team, we give the following six instructions:

1. Review the process alterations needed to reach the VOC that were previously compiled.
2. For each process that has been identified as needing alteration, redraw the process work steps from beginning to end, describing those steps as necessary to achieve the desired result.
3. Mentally test each altered work process for effectiveness and efficiency. (Will this step work? Will it contribute to the desired result?)
4. Identify the kinds of tools (plant, equipment, hand tools, machine tools, hardware, software) that will be needed by workers to perform the altered processes. (More will be said about PET in Chapter 6)
5. Identify the staffing requirements for the altered work processes (number of workers, kind of workers, needed skills).
6. Identify the kind of real-life test that would be needed to ensure that the altered work processes will work.

After this working session, the most important thing the alteration team has to get done is to arrange and conduct the test of the altered processes. Of course, the results of the test may lead to a confirmation or revision of the maps of the altered processes.

ALTER PROCESS MEASURES, GOALS, AND OBJECTIVES TO MATCH THE DIRECTION OF CHANGE

 MIND-CLEARING EXAMPLE

Imagine an actor in a comedy role being transferred to the role of the serious villain in a new play. Imagine the director now saying to the actor, "Remember, your objective on the stage is to make the audience laugh." When questioned by the actor, the director responds, "Yes, we *are* changing the play, but we're not changing any goals at the individual level."

I said earlier that a work process alteration would be involved in some way in every organizational change, but there may be times when the work process steps may not need to be altered if the measures, goals, and objectives of the work processes are altered. I can illustrate this idea with a simple example. Imagine a marketing work process for a company that sells telephone systems. Assume that the following steps are used for identification of prospects in a geographical market:

- Locate chamber of commerce directory for target market.
- Review listings in the directory to identify all companies with sales of 30 million dollars per year.
- Copy addresses, phone numbers, and names of key executives to prospect list.
- Assign market reps to call listed executive names to gather information about their phone needs.

Now let's assume that this company wants to change its strategy to include smaller customers. The work process could be altered by simply changing the size measures of prospect companies from 30 million dollars in annual sales to 5 million dollars. All the work steps would remain essentially the same. No new process maps would need to be drawn.

Use a Team to Identify Needed Alterations in Measures, Goals, and Objectives

We have used the same work process alteration teams to modify measures, goals, and objectives. We use the following four instructions to get the teams focused on the task at hand:

1. Reexamine the process alterations needed to reach the VOC completed in an earlier step.
2. Review those processes where step alterations are *not* needed and answer the following questions:
   - Will we be able to reach the desired VOC if all measures, goals, and objectives remain unchanged?
   - If no, what changes must be made in measures, goals, or objectives for each work process and subprocess?
3. Review those processes where step alterations are needed and answer the following question:
   - What measures, goals, or objectives must be set for each altered work process or subprocess for the VOC to be realized?
4. Label your team's compiled results "Process Performance Measures, Goals, and Objectives Needed to Reach the VOC" and prepare to give team results in the action planning phase that comes later.

ALTER AND TEST WORK PROCEDURES FOR ALTERED PROCESSES

 MIND-CLEARING EXAMPLE

Imagine an actor who asks for written copies of the director's instructions and notes for playing an assigned part and hearing the director say, "Oh, I don't have time to write those down; I'll give you a heads-up if I see you doing something wrong."

Organizations use procedures to guide workers through work processes. A procedure is nothing more that a written set of instructions that describes what workers do with respect to the work processes. In the organizations we have worked with over the years, we have found the widest possible range of procedures in play, from heavily documented, detailed, tightly controlled work instructions for NASA flight controllers, to scrap paper notes taped to machine tools in a manufacturing facility.

People in organizations respond to procedures regardless of the form or rigor of the procedure. Organization members have learned the organization's ways of doing work, and they know from experience that following those ways matters. Therefore, if an organization is changing its work processes, it must also change the procedures that describe that work.

Do we really think that organizations that are trying to change would leave old procedures in play? Yep! All the time! We have seen firsthand managers describing the new ways they want to see their organizations do business while standing in the same room with procedure books that do not reflect those new ways! If you want your organization to change, modify existing procedures to match new processes and publicize them. If the work process alterations in the organization have been extensive, consider conducting training classes on the new procedures for employees.

Testing of new procedures is critical to change. The only way we will know that a new procedure will lead to the right results is to test the newly written procedures with employees who will be expected to use them. We recommend what we call a split test to get the most useful information about a newly written procedure. Identify the test population and split it into two test teams.

1. Give Team 1 a thorough briefing on what you are trying to accomplish with the new procedure and let them follow the new procedure to get their work done. Watch closely to see that the procedure works.

2. Give Team 2 no instructions along with the new procedure. Simply ask them to read the procedure and follow the steps. Watch closely to see how this procedure works. All procedures need to be tested under the no-explanation condition because procedures will eventually find their way into the hands of people who need to use them but who have had no explanation.

Make sure that the new procedures are identified with an effective or revised date. Also consider some special marking, border, or color that catches the workers' eyes and lets them know that new work instructions are in place.

Writing, modifying, and testing the new procedures are the first steps. Marking those procedures as *new* is the next step. The final step is to ensure that every organization member who is to use the procedure gets a copy. The procedure step is not complete until you know that every affected worker has the needed work instructions in hand.

Think about this: if a director is moving his cast of 20 actors to a new play, how many copies of the new script does he need? 20. How many different folks need to get a copy? 20. How does he ensure that each actor has a copy? He hands out 20 on a personal level, or has the stage manager issue them and get signatures. How many signatures? 20. This isn't rocket science, but it is thorough, detailed, specific engineering!

ELIMINATE OLD MEASURES, GOALS, OBJECTIVES, AND PROCEDURES

 MIND-CLEARING EXAMPLE

Imagine a director who allows the master stage copy of the last production script to remain open and in place right beside the master copy of the new play that is currently being performed. When asked about keeping the copy from the old play, imagine the director saying, "No, don't move it. You never know when we might need it again!"

You will be happy to know that commercial airline pilots have mastered change when it comes to new approach procedures. First of all, an approach procedure is a kind of work process that pilots use to approach an airport for landing. Each airport approach is described in a written procedure that pilots carry with them in the cockpit. Following those procedures to the letter is critical for aircraft safety.

Airports periodically change their approaches to reflect needs for better aircraft routing or safety. When they make such a change, new approach procedures are designed, dated, printed, and distributed to all pilots who will use that airport. A standard part of the physical issuance of the new procedures calls for the pilots to turn in their old procedures first. This step is designed to ensure that old, out-of-date procedures will not be used past the effective date of the new ones. Why? Because old procedures left around will get used.

Bottom line, the last critical step in altering work processes for organizational change is to get old work process maps, old procedures, old performance goals out of existence. How do you do that? You systematically collect them and then permanently dispose of them—trash them, shred them, or burn them!

In some situations, where changing to new procedures is especially vital, you might consider holding a formal ceremony to dispose of the old procedures. We have on several occasions worked with clients that had a wake or funeral for old procedures to call special attention to the need to move on to the new way of doing business. While this kind of dramatic step may not be needed for organizations that have mastered change, such steps are clearly important for organizations that are just beginning to become proficient at change. I can see it now, a leader looking over the flames of an old procedure pyre into the eyes of employees mourning the loss of that last crib sheet for getting their jobs done, and seeing them take a deep breath to move on to the new way of doing business!

6

Engineering the Plant, Equipment, and Tools (PET)

 MIND-CLEARING EXAMPLE

Imagine a director who fails to make arrangements to rent the theater for the new production, or who fails to commission workmen to transfer the set and stage rigging from the configuration of the last play to the new one.

The third requirement of engineering organizational change is to alter and test all plant, equipment, and tools (PET) that the organization will need to operate successfully in its new state. For organizational change to happen, there must be physical alteration of the PET used to do work in the organization. PET includes everything from the physical plant where work is done to the equipment and tools required to do the work. PET includes hardware and software. Operating guidelines are the written instructions for proper use and operation of the PET. Failing to alter or supply new PET with the right operating guidelines and still expecting change is akin to expecting a new look to a play that is opening with the old set and old costumes.

The VOC cannot be realized unless the PET needed to support the work processes called for by the vision has been altered, tested, and made available to employees. That is an absolute requirement. In addition, the vision will not be realized until the old PET that is not to be used has been destroyed and removed from the workplace.

Our task in this chapter is to focus on the mechanical alteration of an organization's PET in order to allow the organization to act out the VOC. By virtue of the mechanical nature of organizations, every organizational change may require new PET to enable its work processes. Regardless of the kind of organizational change or the stimulus for organizational change, we work with the assumption that PET alterations will be required unless proven otherwise. We have certainly seen organizational changes that required little or no alteration in PET. As a simple example, imagine a home construction contractor who does framing. Changing the way the frames are put together (i.e., on the job or off the job) will require major alterations to work steps involved, but requires no changes in the hammers used by the framing carpenters. On the other hand, this same framing contractor might need to change the equipment used to bring completed, bulky frames to the job site instead of compact bundles of lumber.

Change Requires PET Alterations

While the obvious case for altering PET comes when new PET is the organization's change goal from the beginning, other cases requiring alterations of PET are driven by very different kinds of change motivations. For example:

- If an organization decides to change its business strategy to become the low-cost producer, many, if not all, of the organization's production processes will need to change to take out costly manufacturing steps or to alter the sequence of steps, and so on. Altering any parts of the manufacturing work process is likely to require a different plant configuration and work tools.
- If an organization decides to reengineer one of its work processes in order to achieve new efficiencies, tool changes might be required to support altered steps in the work process. As tool changes are made, corresponding changes might be needed in the written operating guidelines that support those tools.
- If an organization decides to make a change in its culture (i.e., the way we do things around here), several process changes will result as organization members begin to approach their jobs differently. For example, if the desired cultural change is to become more attentive to customers, changes will probably need to be made in the steps used in customer service departments or help desks. As

alterations are made in customer service steps, modifications are likely to be required in the tools used by customer service employees, namely software applications and telecommunications equipment.

The requirement to alter the organization's PET is one of the best-handled components of organizational change and one of the worst. For what we call visible PET—physical plant, machine tools, and even hand tools—alterations are usually very well done. We think this kind of change is handled so well because these types of PET are easy to see. Failure to alter these kinds of PET would be easy to spot and correct. We have also noted that most changes in big PET such as factories and plants are handled by trained engineers and construction managers who tackle alteration or modification as an engineering problem.

But where the PET to be altered is invisible, it is frequently not handled as well. For example, alteration of software to accommodate changes seems much tougher to deal with. First, it is not easy to see. Second, its alteration is usually not handled by people with an engineering mindset. Our approach for dealing with the software issue is covered later in this chapter.

IDENTIFY THE PET ALTERATIONS NEEDED FOR CHANGE

 MIND-CLEARING EXAMPLE

Imagine a director who selects a new play and who commits to an opening date without working through the modifications that will need to be made to the props and backdrops for staging the play.

The purpose of this step is to identify those physical alterations that will be needed in the organization's PET so that work can be done on them to meet the organization's schedule for change. To have any hope of making an organization successfully change, we must know with as much certainty as possible the construction or modification tasks that must be completed before the VOC can be fully realized.

We have been successful in identifying needed alterations to an organization's PET with two different approaches: (1) the PET inventory approach and (2) the process inventory approach. The PET inventory approach is the most logical to use when the organizational change is being driven primarily by desire for new PET. The process inventory approach is the most logical for all other kinds of organizational changes.

Approach 1:
Identify PET Alterations
with a PET Inventory

Some organizations focus directly on changing PET as a way of better meeting their organizational goals. For example, a chemical company may focus on getting a new reactor installed because they believe it will have a higher conversion efficiency, thereby increasing the amount of usable product from manufacturing. Installing new PET almost always starts a ripple effect of needed work on existing PET to physically accommodate the new PET. For example, the new process reactor mentioned above may need more electrical power than the reactor it will replace.

The bottom line fact associated with the installation of new PET is very simple. It is easy and commonplace to overlook changes that are needed in existing PET to accommodate the new PET. Over the years, we have seen many organizational changes delayed because the new PET had an unexpected and unplanned ripple effect on neighboring equipment. We have seen unanticipated power drains that impact other equipment. We have seen many heating and cooling problems emerge because of new equipment operating in ways that differed from what was planned, and so on.

This step of identifying needed PET alterations can be anything from a huge project (if you are acquiring a new plant) to a short and sweet exercise (if the acquisition is something as simple as a hand tool). One of the easiest ways to identify PET alterations is to convene a team made up of technical folks who know the organization's PET and employees who will use the new PET or work in the physical location that will be its home. We give the team the following six instructions:

1. Study the VOC and understand what is being done and why.
2. Study the plans, blueprints, drawings, and specifications for the new PET and identify alterations needed in present PET.

3. Find additional needed alterations in existing PET by conducting a walk-through inspection of the work area that will receive the new PET. Identify direct connections that will need to be made between new and existing PET. Direct connections include physical structures and utilities. In addition, look for changes in the indirect connections or impacts that may require alterations in existing PET (heat, ventilation, air-conditioning, space, noise, health, safety and environment, etc.).

4. Study the plans, blueprints, drawings, and specifications for the existing PET that will need to be altered to discover additional alterations that were not visible in the walk-through inspection.

5. Compile the results of your team's deliberations into the following categories:
   - PET that needs alteration.
   - The kind and nature of alteration needed for each piece of PET.

6. Label your team's compiled results "PET Alterations Needed to Reach the VOC" and prepare to give team results during action planning.

   The kinds of alterations that could appear on the PET alteration team's list might be as follows:
   - Move a warehouse wall back two feet to accommodate a new cooling duct.
   - Add two more electrical junction boxes for the west wall of a factory.
   - Upgrade all modems in Department B to 56k baud.
   - Provide leather gloves for all operators in Department C.

This approach sounds straightforward and simple enough, but it is not. In reality, the PET alteration team will need to repeat the above exercise at least two more times: during the installation of the newly acquired PET and after installation is complete. Our experience over 30 years is that additional needed alterations in the organization's existing PET will continue to be found right through installation and use, and sometimes even months or years later.

Approach 2:
Identify PET Alterations
with a Process Inventory

Use of this approach to identify needed alterations in PET assumes that the reason for the organizational change is something other than

PET driven. Many alterations in PET are needed because the organization starts to change its strategy, work processes, or the behavior and performance of its employees. For example, a company that wants to lower its manufacturing costs might change an assembly process that requires a change from using screws to rivets, requiring changes from power screwdrivers to rivet guns. Moving to rivets might also require that holes for rivets be drilled with a different tool than starter holes for screws.

We have found that one of the easiest ways to identify PET alterations is to convene a team that has three different perspectives: (1) employees intimately involved in identifying work process changes, (2) technical folks who know the organization's PET, and (3) employees who will use the new or altered PET. We give the team the following nine instructions:

1. Study the VOC and understand what is being done and why.
2. Study the alterations that will be made in the work processes in order to enact. (The compiled report from the process alteration team is invaluable here.)
3. Visualize the PET that will be needed to support the work processes that will enact the VOC. Identify both new PET that will need to be acquired and existing PET that will need to be altered.
4. Obtain copies of plans, blueprints, drawings, and specifications for the new PET and identify alterations needed in present PET.
5. Find additional needed alterations in existing PET by conducting a walk-through inspection of the work area that will receive the new PET. Identify direct and indirect connections that will need to be made between new and existing PET.
6. Conduct a second walk-through along process lines. Follow the path of the organization's product or service from start to end of production and identify the kind of PET that will be needed.
7. Study the plans, blueprints, drawings, and specifications for the existing PET that will need to be altered to discover additional alterations that were not visible in the walk-through inspection.
8. Compile the results of your team's deliberations into the following categories:
   • PET that needs alteration.
   • The kind and nature of alteration needed for each piece of PET.
9. Label your team's compiled results "PET Alterations Needed to Reach VOC" and prepare to give team results during action planning.

As in the first approach to identifying required changes in PET, this second approach also will need to be repeated during and after PET installation and testing. Regardless of the approach used, change managers need to approach this engineering task for what it is—a specific, detailed, comprehensive design. Many organizational changes have gone awry because the change planners did not take the time to comprehensively review all of their organization's PET and specifically identify the alteration work that was needed for the change.

A Very Special Case: The Alteration of Software

Software is PET—a very important part of PET. Rarely do organizational changes these days not involve some information technology system. Everything that I have said so far about altering PET applies to software and systems. But many times the organization members involved in the alteration of PET are different when software is involved. That's good news and bad news!

When we talk to information technology professionals about altering software, they immediately translate what we are saying into the vocabulary of their profession. Their translation becomes "application development or modification." In many organizations there are information technology (IT) professionals who specialize in *aps* or *AD*. These professionals already have approaches or techniques they use to develop or modify an IT application. The first step in their usual approach is frequently called *defining requirements*. Depending on the size of your organization, you may have IT professionals who specialize in defining requirements for applications' development or modification. And therein lie the good and bad news.

We have found it very difficult to intervene in a requirements definition process. Most IT professionals who do requirements definition are focused professionals using a disciplined approach to identify and record what users want their new or modified information system to do. That's the good news. A professional using a systematic approach can help you identify the alterations that need to be made to your software PET.

The bad news is that frequently the IT professional does not receive a really good picture of the organizational change that is driving the system alteration. This inadequate or incomplete picture can occur because the users who are interviewed by the IT professional do not have or convey a good picture of the vision, or because of the narrow focus of the IT professional who is only listening for technical inputs to the applications development or modification process.

Regardless of the reason for the problem, the change leader must take control of the requirement definition situation to ensure that the software alterations that are identified accurately reflect the PET changes needed to reach the VOC. We have found the following seven steps to be useful for the change leader when working with the IT professional in requirements definition:

1. Meet with the IT professional and explain the organizational change that is driving the need for software alteration.
2. Go over in as much detail as you can the VOC.
3. Go over in detail the work process alterations that are being made to accommodate the organizational change. Go over the entire work process change, not just the parts to be automated.
4. Work with the IT professionals to identify who will be interviewed to identify user requirements for the software alteration. (It clearly helps to have members of the process alteration team be a part of the population to be interviewed.)
5. Have the IT professional walk through any requirements definition approach with you. (This approach will largely consist of questions that he will use in his interviews with the users.) Identify the questions in the approach that best address the PET alteration needs as you understand them.
6. Thank the IT professional for helping your change effort, then get out of the way while the work is done.
7. When the IT professional completes his requirements definition task, sit down and review the results. Ensure as best you can that the requirements as defined will lead to software alterations that will contribute to the VOC. And don't be surprised if what you find leads to additional interviews between you, the organization's end users, and the IT professional.

If you use the suggestions above, you will have done about all you can do with the IT end of the organizational change. Then just hope that what comes will be altered software that helps you keep your organizational change on target, on time, and on budget.

ALTER AND TEST PET
CRITICAL TO THE CHANGE

 MIND-CLEARING EXAMPLE

Imagine a stage manager who gets a list of the needed scene changes for the new play, but tells the puzzled stagehands not to change anything from the last play. Or imagine the lighting director asking a technician if all the spotlights had been changed over to the new required colors and being happy with the following answer, "Well, I changed three of the five."

By this time the change leader should have clearly identified both the new PET needed for the impending change and the alterations that will be needed for existing PET. In this step, the change leader now needs to ensure that all the needed PET work gets done satisfactorily. In addition, he must ensure that all new and altered PET has been thoroughly tested to ensure that it operates as it needs to in order to support the VOC.

To a large degree, the change leader's success in making needed alterations in PET will be dependent on his organization's capability in two important management areas: (1) construction and (2) software management. Getting needed alteration of PET (not software) will be dependent on how well the organization executes the principles in the discipline of construction management. Getting needed alteration of software PET will largely be dependent on the organization's maturity or development level in software processes.

Alteration of Physical PET

Some form of construction management must be used to have any chance of successfully installing new PET or altering existing PET (assuming that we are talking about something more than going to a hardware store and picking up a new claw hammer). The underlying theme in this book is that organizations are first and foremost mechanical systems that have physical attributes to be altered to achieve organizational change. These physical attributes—work processes, performance management systems, and PET—can all be altered with precision if the construction management discipline is applied.

The change leaders in the organization must themselves have a common sense construction management mindset. Almost every manager in today's organizations has at least some passing experience with construction management or equipment installation, or they are veterans of some construction project around their homes. They are likely to have been assigned to manage a construction project (remodel an office or buy/install a new copier), or they have been around while such a project was being worked. They have probably seen the common sense of construction management:

- Get a clear understanding of what you are trying to do with the construction project.
- Clarify the construction budget and general time schedules if available.
- Decide which equipment needs to be bought or altered.
- Contact vendors who sell or modify that equipment.
- Let vendors know what you want and get a proposal/bid from them.
- Evaluate the proposals and choose the vendor(s).
- Lay out the work of the vendor(s) on a time schedule.
- Calculate the total construction dollars likely to be involved.
- Secure management approval of the budget and schedule.
- Get vendors under contract and started on the job.
- Monitor vendor progress and manage problems day to day to ensure the successful completion of the project on target, on time, and on budget.
- Close out the project with the equipment users, ensuring that their needs have been met, and ensure that the contractors have been paid and have left the premises.

Change leaders can put construction management into play in PET alteration in any of the three following ways, and their choice of a way or approach should be based on the size and complexity of the construction (or the *alteration* as we have named it).

1. *Use common sense construction management.* For small or simple purchases or installations, it may be OK to use nothing more

than the common sense approach, but it must be done in a very disciplined way with goals, schedules, and so on.

2. *Engage an internal manager who is experienced in construction management.* Construction is not new for most organizations that have a history of growth and expansion. Many organizations have qualified professionals on board who can become the construction manager for acquiring and installing the new tools and machinery associated with organizational change.

3. *Engage a construction management company (or professional) from the outside.* Some organizations prefer to use outside construction resources for large and/or complicated processes. You may be aware that there is an entire industry called *engineering and construction* whose mission it is to design, procure, and construct major capital projects.

Alteration of Software PET

The process of buying, developing or modifying software PET will usually be handled by the organization's information technology department. IT departments in most companies are accustomed to handling such changes. But from the perspective of engineering change, what counts is the IT department's overall competence to handle software change in an orderly predictable way that will allow our change initiative to be on target, on time, and on budget.

The Software Engineering Institute of Carnegie Mellon University talks about the overall capability of IT organizations to manage software processes. They talk about IT organizations with *immature* software processes versus those with *mature* software processes.

In an immature software organization, software processes are generally improvised by practitioners and their management during the course of the project. Even if a software process has been specified, it is not rigorously followed or enforced. The immature software organization is reactionary, and managers are usually focused on solving immediate crises (better known as fire fighting). Schedules and budgets are routinely exceeded because they are not based on realistic estimates. When hard deadlines are imposed, product functionality and quality are often compromised to meet the schedule.

On the other hand, a mature software organization possesses an organization-wide ability for managing software development and maintenance processes. The software process is accurately communicated to both existing staff and new employees, and work activities are carried out according to the planned process. The processes mandated are fit for use and consistent with the way the work actually gets done. These defined processes are updated when necessary, and improvements are developed through controlled pilot-tests and/or cost benefit analyses. Roles and responsibilities within the defined process are clear throughout the project and across the organization.

In a mature organization, managers monitor the quality of the software products and customer satisfaction . . . schedules and budgets are based on historical performance and are realistic; the expected results for cost, schedule, functionality, and quality of the product are usually achieved. (Technical Report SEI-93-TR-24)

In our quest to make changes happen on target, on time, and on budget, it is easy to see how alteration of PET might be a weak link in change if those alterations were being done by an IT organization with immature software processes. Our recommendations for handling different levels of maturity and different degrees of needed alteration are shown in very general form in Figure 6.1.

Figure 6.1 is probably clear enough to send the strong message that IT maturity is a requirement for altering software that is to be a part of an organizational change intended to be on target, on time, and on budget. For simple, small changes done in-house in an immature IT organization, it is important to get the very best IT resources in the organization on the software alteration project. Odds are they will not use systematic software processes, but they probably will do the best job in the IT organization of improvising the software solution.

Testing of New and Altered PET

Just as we wanted to test altered processes, we must test new or altered PET to ensure that it will be ready to play its part in the organizational change. If you use the key principles of construction management and mature software processes in altering the physical PET, testing of the final PET and its installation will be done as a part of the project closeout. Sounds like an easy-enough answer to our testing requirement, doesn't it?

FIGURE 6.1 Recommendations for Resourcing Software Alteration

Software Alteration

		Simple and Small	Big and Complex
IT Organization	**Mature**	Use In-House IT Resources	Consider Using In-House Resources Supplemented by Mature Outside Vendor
	Immature	Do with In-House Resources Only If You Use the Best IT Performers	Use Mature Outside Vendor Only

Beware of testing done at the closeout of the project, whether it be for physical or software PET. Those are needed tests and they likely will be done right as part of a disciplined alteration, but they don't go far enough. What is needed are tests of the PET in the context of the actual work processes that require those particular tools. Our recommendation is to use members of the work process alteration and PET alteration teams to conduct a real-life test of the PET using the altered processes defined earlier. A further step would be to use employees who will actually be using the PET with the altered process when the intended change is finally put into effect.

Tests of the altered PET almost always produce observations from the test participants that point to further alteration of the PET. Change leaders will need to differentiate between those suggested alterations that are learning-curve based or preferences/styles based rather than process-requirements based. Learning-curve based suggestions may be driven more by the test subjects' unfamiliarity with the PET than with actual PET inadequacy. If you discover major needed alterations at this point, you haven't been doing something right.

ALTER AND TEST PET CONTROLS

MIND-CLEARING EXAMPLE

Imagine a lighting director who ensures that all the right lights are in place and focused on the stage but does not alter or test the lighting control panel that is still set up for the last production.

So far we have altered processes and purchased or altered and tested the PET required for those processes. The next step is for the change leader to ensure that the controls on the PET will allow the performance called for by the work process. PET controls are those devices that allow the operators of the PET to make the equipment do what it needs to do, when it needs to do it, in order to perform the work called for by work processes. Sometimes limitations are set on PET controls that limit the overall performance of the PET.

A simple real-world example of PET control is the accelerator pedal on a truck. Some trucks have a device installed on the engine called a governor that artificially limits the speed of the truck to some speed well within the truck's operating limits. If the driver's work process is changed to require a higher speed than the one set on the governor, he will not be able to control the truck to meet the new process requirements.

The job of the change leader is to ensure that control devices on altered equipment are adjusted to meet new process requirements, and that control devices on new equipment provide the operating envelope needed by the work process. While the PET test that we conducted in the previous step will pick up control limitations on the specific PET tested, all duplicate equipment will need to be physically inspected to ensure it is set within the needed operating parameters.

ALTER PET GUIDELINES TO MATCH THE IMPENDING CHANGE

 MIND-CLEARING EXAMPLE

Imagine a lighting director who refuses to allow the lighting technicians to put any of their complicated lighting limitations down on paper. Imagine the lighting director saying, "Don't worry about writing all this stuff down, you'll get it after a few performances!"

Organizations use operating guidelines to guide workers through the proper use of PET. An operating guideline is nothing more than a written set of instructions that describes what workers should and should not do in operation of a particular piece of PET. Operating guidelines are usually provided by the original equipment manufactures (OEM) of the PET. Before I talk about the alteration of operating guidelines, let's look at an example of guidelines and the work procedures that use that equipment to avoid any confusion between the two terms.

The copier in our office has the following two operating guidelines attached to the top of the machine:

1. Do not replenish toner before the "Add Toner" lamp flashes.
2. When replenishing toner, add only one cartridge of toner.

Meanwhile, we have two work procedures that involve the use of that copier:

1. Always record the number of copies produced in the copier log immediately after copying.
2. Record the client billing code and date used right beside the number of copies made.

In the organizations we have worked with over the years, we have found a wide range of operating guidelines in play. For some PET, we have seen extensive operating guidelines, usually provided by the OEM, while others have only three lines of operating instructions fixed to the equipment itself.

The important thing about operating guidelines is not necessarily how many there are but how usable they are. We have found that most operating guidelines provided by OEM are not only skimpy and poorly written, but user unfriendly! The exception to this general finding is an OEM that produces PET that has a possible loss of life associated with it. In those cases, operating guidelines are much more clearly written and user friendly.

Most companies develop additional operating guidelines beyond those produced by the OEM. Sometimes these additional operating guidelines are written down, but unfortunately, most times they are not. So around existing PET there is frequently an unwritten body of operating guidelines that are important to the organization's knowledge of how to use the PET.

Amid this environment of poorly written instructions and unwritten guidelines, leaders of a change initiative must still divine a way to make change happen on target, on time and on budget. Therefore, there are two critical challenges for dealing with PET operating guidelines:

1. *For new PET, supplement the OEM operating guidelines with your organization's standard additions.* This means that the operating guidelines that come with the newly purchased PET should not be accepted as all that is needed. As a part of the installation and testing of the new PET, make it a priority to write additional operating instructions as needed to raise the guidelines to the standard that your organization already provides on existing PET.

2. *For existing PET that needs to be altered, change the operating guidelines in writing.* If the impending organizational change calls for the modification of existing PET, the task to get operating guidelines in order will be to document the written and unwritten guidelines already in use for the PET before modification. Then rewrite those guidelines for the altered equipment. We have found it effective to write the new guidelines on the same document, visibly crossing out the guidelines no longer to be used.

Testing operating guidelines for new PET and altered guidelines for existing PET is critical to change. The only way you will know that new guidelines will lead to the right results is to test the newly written guidelines with employees from the populations that will be expected to use them. We recommend a split test to get the most useful information about operating guidelines. Identify the test population and split it into two test teams.

1. Give Team 1 a thorough briefing on what you are trying to accomplish with the new operating guidelines and then let them demonstrate how they would use the new guidelines on the PET. Watch closely to see that the demonstration coincides with your intention for the PET.

2. Give Team 2 no additional instructions to go along with the new operating guidelines. Simply ask them to read the guidelines and demonstrate how they would follow them. Watch closely to see how the new guidelines work. All operating guidelines need to be tested under the no-explanation condition because guidelines will eventually find their way into the hands of people who need to use them but who have had no explanation.

Make sure that the new operating guidelines are identified with an effective or a revised date. Also consider some special marking, border, or color that catches the workers' eyes and lets them know that new operating guidelines are in place. Once again, new guidelines are of no value unless you get them into the hands of the people who will need to use them in their day-to-day work.

ELIMINATE OLD PET AND OPERATING GUIDELINES

 MIND-CLEARING EXAMPLE

Imagine a lighting director who instructs her technicians to leave the taped lighting level marks from the last production on the lighting panels next to the new marks. Or imagine a stage manager who leaves all of the props from the last play in the prop racks along with the new props.

The bottom line for this requirement of engineering PET is simple to say but more difficult to follow: you must get equipment you no longer want to use *out* of the organization. The undesired PET must be destroyed or put where people can't get their hands on it—or it will be used.

The bottom line for operating guidelines is equally simple but much harder to follow. Essentially you want to eliminate operating guidelines that are no longer relevant, needed, or correct. This simple task is complicated by the fact that many of the operating guidelines in use are not written down. It is always tough to get a written policy, procedure, or guideline out of play. It is especially difficult to get something unwritten out of play! But it can be done. We recommend the following seven steps:

1. Identify the PET operating guidelines that you want to eliminate.
2. Draft a written version of those guidelines (using what is already written along with information from folks who know the unwritten rules).
3. Give everybody a copy of the written version.
4. Call everyone's attention to the written version.
5. Tell everyone that the old operating guidelines will no longer be used.
6. Take the old copies away from them.
7. Destroy the copies in front of everyone.

The commercial airline pilots I mentioned in Chapter 5 not only systematically deal with changes in work processes and procedures; they also deal with changes in the operating guidelines for the equipment on the aircraft they fly on a daily basis. Not only do pilots systematically remove all old operating guidelines from their flight reference guides, but they systematically examine the cockpits of the aircraft to ensure that there are no lingering operating guidelines present. They have learned from experience that following an old operating guide can lead to disaster.

7

Engineering the Performance Management System

The fourth requirement of engineering organizational change is to alter the guiding direction in the performance management system to reinforce the transition to the new organizational future and discourage failure during transition to the new future. For organizational change to happen, there must be physical alteration of the system that you use to direct and reinforce the performance of managers and employees. This *performance management system* is the organization's mechanism for procuring, directing, and retaining the kind of performance it needs. For successful organizational change, employees must be "under contract" to perform to the new vision of the organization. In addition, all employees must be under contract for the *transition* to the new vision, performing normal, routine duties while changing to the new vision. Failing to alter the performance management system while expecting change is akin to expecting the performance of a new play from actors still under exclusive contract to perform the old play.

THE PERFORMANCE MANAGEMENT SYSTEM

After 30 years of consulting work with organizations that were trying to change, we can categorically state that the biggest obstacle to change—on target, on time, and on budget—is the way managers handle the people of the organization. Altering the organization's physical PET seems to be the part of organizational change done best, while altering the performance management system for the people of the organization seems to be the most difficult by far.

There are two classic performance management systems that organizations use to steer the behavior of the people they employ. The first system, *contractor or vendor management,* is used for steering the behavior of those persons whom the company considers outside contractors or vendors. The second mechanism, *employee performance management,* is used for steering the behavior of those persons whom the organization considers full- or part-time employees.

Managing Contractor Performance

The contractor system includes such critical and logical steps as:

- Defining the desired work the company wants from a contractor/vendor.
- Locating, negotiating, and reaching agreement with a contractor who can do the desired work.
- Explaining the work to be done to the vendor and ensuring understanding.
- Familiarizing the vendor with the way the company works.
- Authorizing the vendor to begin work.
- Monitoring vendor performance over time.
- Ensuring that the vendor has completed the required work and is paid in accordance with the negotiated agreement.

The primary administrative vehicle used in this process is a written contract. This instrument, signed by both the vendor and the organization, contains key sections that are necessary to ensure desired performance of the vendor:

- *Statement of Work.* This statement identifies precisely what the contractor is to do for the hiring company during the specified time period.
- *Qualifications.* These specify what skills and capabilities the contractor is required to bring to the assignment.
- *Performance Evaluation.* This evaluation tells the contractor how performance will be measured, monitored, and evaluated.
- *Payment.* You must spell out the agreed-to payment for the desired work.
- *General Terms.* These describe how the contractor and organization will do business together during the contract period.

Contracting for vendor performance is normally handled by the organization's procurement function or human resources. The day-to-day management of the vendor is usually handled by an operating manager who is employing the vendor's services in designated work. This employing manager directs the vendor's performance as necessary within the scope and arrangements of the contract.

As the work needs of the organization change, the employing manager works with the contracting officer and the vendor to modify and renegotiate the vendor contract. The employing manager works in this fashion, keeping the vendor and the contract aligned with the work requirements of the organization until there is no longer a need for the services of the contractor. At completion of the agreed-to work, the contract is terminated and the vendor and the organization go their separate ways.

Managing Employee Performance

In theory, employee performance is managed very much like contractor performance. An employee must be under contract to do the work of the organization in order to receive the rewards for work. When we use the term *contract* with employees, we are usually not talking about the written contract that is used with vendors. In practice, very few employees have a written contract. But all employees work under an agreement with the company—the equivalent of a contract. Employees understand that they are to do certain things for the company in order to be paid.

The steps you take to get employees under agreement and to work for the company are similar to the steps you take with contractors. You must systematically and responsibly take the following seven interrelated steps:

1. Think through what work you want the employees to do.
2. Find employees who have the skills, capabilities, and initiative necessary to do that work.
3. Communicate the work to the employees and secure their understanding and willingness to do the work (at this point the employees are under agreement).
4. Provide any final training needed by the employees to be able to do their work.
5. Have the employees begin work, including taking personal initiative to perform to the needed level in their new roles.
6. Ensure the employees get feedback on how their work is progressing.
7. Evaluate employee performance and ensure the employees are properly/fairly paid for their services.

Our key message is a simple one: for long-term success in employee performance management, employees must always stay under agreement to do the work of the company. And as the requirements of the work change, it is up to the employing manager to keep an up-to-date agreement in effect at all times.

For example, let's say that an employee has been under agreement to do tasks *A* through *F* in a company department. Let's say that the work needed in that department changes, for whatever reason. It is up to the employing manager to get the employee under agreement to do the new work—say, tasks *B* through *H*. The employing manager follows the steps shown above: understanding the new work; communicating the new work to the employee; gaining his understanding and agreement to start two new tasks, stop doing one old task, and continue doing the remainder of the old tasks; providing training as needed for the new tasks; starting the new employee to work on the new tasks; providing feedback to the employee on performance; and ensuring that the employee's performance is fully evaluated at the end of the year and that the employee is properly paid for doing the new job and not the old one.

As in the case of vendor management, the employing manager works with representatives of the human resources unit for assistance in completing the basic steps in managing employee performance.

While the details may vary from company to company, it is critical for employing managers and human resource managers to come to clear agreement on how they will work together to ensure effective and efficient performance management.

That is the big picture on performance management. Now we look at the individual steps to engineer the performance management system for an organizational change: altering individual roles and goals, getting workers under agreement, making sure they have been trained for their future roles, arranging for feedback to employees, and paying the salaries of those workers who make the change.

IDENTIFY AND ALTER INDIVIDUAL ROLES AND GOALS NEEDED FOR CHANGE

 MIND-CLEARING EXAMPLE

Imagine a director who can't decide how many dancers will be in the chorus line for his new musical. Imagine the director responds to one of the dancers, "I don't know if you will be in the line or not. Just work your way in somewhere and we'll see what develops." Or imagine a director who has decided she wants a certain actor in the new production but is unwilling to decide which of three roles might be the best use of the actor's talent.

We use an organization's performance management system to reinforce the work that managers and employees will need to do for an organizational change to be effective. This step in engineering the performance management system is all about identifying the specific roles and goals that workers will need to develop and use after an organizational change. Just as each actor in a performance must have a role, so must each employee. We define *role* as an organization member's assigned set of tasks and responsibilities. (From our earlier discussion of performance management, an employee's role is the agreed-to statement of work that the employee is paid to accomplish.)

In addition to role descriptions, workers need specific targets or goals for designated time periods. We want to set specific goals and objectives for individual and team performance needed to meet the process objectives already set in the second requirement—altering work processes. We want to have specific measures that can be monitored by both workers and managers to understand and manage the level of worker performance.

Change Requires New or Altered Roles and Goals

The job for the change leader is first and foremost to identify what roles will be needed to fulfill the VOC. She then must identify the goals that need to be associated with each role to meet the level of performance expected in the vision. Then the change leader must identify which new roles will be needed (with accompanying goals), which existing roles will need to change (and the direction of those changes), and which roles will *not* change, and then to communicate that information to everybody in the organization. This sounds simple, and it is. But it can become a big job because some organizations have many managers and employees to fit into new roles or to steady in old roles.

Regardless of the kind of organizational change or the stimulus for organizational change, new roles and goals or alterations of some existing roles and goals will be required.

- If an organization decides to *change its business strategy* to become the low-cost producer, for example, many, if not all, of the organization's production processes will need to change to take out costly manufacturing steps or to alter the sequence of steps, and so on. In addition, the company's marketing and sales processes will need to be altered to add selling steps and promotional materials that stress changed features of the organization's products. This kind of strategy change will require that people do things differently (i.e., have their roles and goals altered) in accordance with the new work processes.
- If an organization decides to *change one of the tools* that it uses in its business, role and goal alterations almost certainly will be involved. Work steps to set up the new tool and to use the output of the new tool will need to be assigned to somebody (i.e., become a part of their role in the company). A new software tool, for instance, likely will require either new data elements to enter the

software and/or new steps to use the output of the software, requiring alteration of the roles and goals of the assigned workers.

- If an organization decides to *change its culture,* several process changes will result as organization members begin to approach their jobs differently. For example, if the desired cultural change is to become more attentive to customers, changes probably will need to be made in the steps used in customer service departments or help desks, impacting the roles and goals of the organization members assigned to those departments. We believe that the primary tool for changing an organization's culture is the performance management system. Culture change begins with the revision of employee roles to include the desired behaviors wanted in the new culture.

- If an organization decides to *change its organizational structure,* alterations likely will be required both in management/decision-making processes and the work processes performed by members of the units involved. These process alterations will result in role alterations for managers and workers alike. (Note: In over 30 years of consulting, we have seen companies make many changes to their organization structures that were entirely superficial in nature, leading to no substantial changes to the four mechanical attributes emphasized in this book. To us, an organization change should be focused on bringing better resourcing of people and skills to bear on substantial changes to work processes. In short, we tell our customers to forget about changing the organization structure if they do not intend to make work processes more effective or efficient.)

This first step in engineering the organization's performance management system is to identify a role and goal for everybody in the changing organization. Everyone must have an identified new work role and goal for performance after the organization does its change. For many organizational changes, the roles and goals of some employees will remain unchanged.

Use a Team to Identify New and Altered Organizational Roles and Goals

You want to finish this step with three end products: (1) a list of the new roles that will be needed; (2) a list of the roles that will need to be altered, along with the direction/nature of the required alteration; and

(3) a list of the organizational roles that will not need to be altered to enact the vision. We generate these lists from analysis of four resources:

1. List of work processes to be altered.
2. List of PET to be altered.
3. The organization chart and accompanying tables.
4. The organization's master listing of personnel.

The first step in identifying needed role and goal alterations (and/or new roles) is to systematically go through the organization's work processes and PET to visualize any modifications that will be needed in roles and goals for organization members. In previous steps—alteration of work processes (Chapter 5) and alteration of PET (Chapter 6)—we generated lists entitled "Process Alterations Needed to Reach the VOC" and "PET Alterations Needed to Reach the VOC." These lists are the obvious starting places for identifying role and goal alterations or new roles.

One of the easiest ways to identify needed role and goal alterations and new roles and goals is to convene a team of employees that knows the organization very well and knows the details of the work process alterations that are needed. Have that team go through the two alteration lists (work process and PET) to look for contacts with organization members. We give the team the following eight instructions:

1. Spend 15 minutes getting as clear as you can on the vision.
2. Study the work process alteration list.
3. Note any PET alterations that go with the alterations in work processes.
4. Superimpose the firm's organization charts over the work processes that need to be altered to get a feel for which existing worker roles will be involved with altered processes.
5. Answer the following questions for each work process listed as needing alteration:
   - Which employee roles touch the work processes to be altered?
   - How will the roles of those employees who touch the work process need to be altered? (i.e., How should their roles be modified to cause them to perform to the needed level in the work processes using the needed PET?)
   - What goals and objectives must be met by workers in the altered roles?

- What totally new roles will be needed in order to get all the work of the altered processes done?
- What goals and objectives must be met by workers in the new roles?
- Which roles will need to work together as work teams to get the needed level of performance?
- What goals and objectives must be met by each needed work team?

6. Next, as a check to the step you have just completed, go through the organization's existing organization charts/table and the list of all employees. For each position and for each person, answer the following question:
   - Will this existing position/person be involved in the altered work processes or the altered PET?
   - If yes, add that name to the list of roles to be altered along with the nature of the needed role alteration
   - If no, add that name to the list of roles that will not need to be altered.

7. Compile the results of your team's deliberations and label it "Role Alterations Needed to Reach the VOC." Organize the list in the following categories:
   - New roles and goals needed to perform work processes.
   - Existing roles and goals that need to be altered.
   - Direction of each role that needs to be altered.
   - Teams that will need to work together to perform the altered processes along with team goals.
   - Existing roles that will not need to be altered.

8. Label your team's compiled results "New Roles and Existing Role Alterations Needed to Reach the VOC" and prepare to give team results during action planning.

For more complicated or comprehensive organizational changes, the structure of the organization chart might need to be altered to give the best structure to the individual teams and roles. Without going into great detail on organizational design, we want to identify the way we will organize units—individuals and teams—around the work to perform efficiently to the VOC.

Support Workers as They Develop
Needed Roles and Goals

Organizations that have mastered change expect that workers will take the needed initiative to develop their new or altered roles when cued by their bosses to do so. A boss must make it a given that her workers will exercise the personal leadership needed to develop new roles to accommodate needed organizational change.

Experience has taught us that change leaders need to orchestrate the process to ensure that all workers have their needed role and goal alterations identified and made. Failure to use a firm hand to ensure that such work gets done will inevitably produce great variance in scheduled completion of the alteration (many workers will be late if left to their own devices) as well as great variation in the thoroughness and level of detail of role description and documentation.

An approach that has worked for us for years is a simple one. We encourage old pro employees to develop their own needed role and goal alterations with little assistance from the boss. On the other hand, we recommend that the boss takes the lead in developing the roles of rookie employees who are new to the work of the company. Regardless of who works through the alterations, those alterations still need to be done on schedule for the change to happen as expected.

In the end, it is each individual worker who will have to work through the details of her role and goals in order to meet the expectations of the organization after the change. But change leaders do need to take firm control of the process of identifying and ensuring role and goal alterations to have any real chance to have the organizational change—on target, on time, and on budget.

Document the New and
Altered Roles and Goals

Companies vary in the way they handle the contents of roles of organization members. Some companies have written roles and goals for their positions and some do not. While there is great variation among companies, the most popular device for recording the contents of roles is a job description with an accompanying annual goals list. Our bottom line is simple: we don't really care what kind of device the company uses to document roles as long as there is such a device and it is used systematically. The written job description with accompanying goals for the new and altered roles is the equivalent of the new statement of work that will be expected from vendors or employees after the changeover.

Determine the Compensation Level for New and Altered Roles

The last critical part of the role alteration step is to determine the compensation level that matches the new and altered roles needed for the vision. It will do no good to offer an employee an altered role if the offered compensation is not enough to get the employee to accept it. This critical step must be initiated by the change leader assisted by a representative from human resources. That HR representative must ensure that the altered roles and the determined compensation for those roles fit with the company's normal human resources compensation policy and procedures.

- *No compensation change for typical role alteration.* If the altered role still fits within the same job classification (and labor market), the organization should not need to change compensation for the role. In fact, one of our key goals in identifying needed role alterations is to keep jobs within the same families and classification ranges.
- *No pay for routine change.* We cannot give extra compensation— a raise or a bonus—for a normal change in an organization. If a company were forced to pay everyone for every change, that company would soon find itself with a cost structure that was out of line with the marketplace. A key idea is that once organizations and individuals have mastered change, they will both be willing and able to make normal changes without a great deal of support and attention, and without feeling that extra compensation is due.
- *Pay for role alterations that significantly change the employment situation.* Occasionally, when organizations alter jobs so that more or higher-level skills are involved in the new work, it may be necessary to pay for those new skills through a change in the employee's compensation package. Some companies, for example, have procedures for grading jobs on difficulty, the amount of accountability for results, the number of people supervised, etc. If role alterations move an employee to a new salary classification level, the company will need to be prepared to pay for it.

COMPLETE ONE-ON-ONE CONTRACTING FOR EVERY AFFECTED PERSON

 MIND-CLEARING EXAMPLE

Imagine a director who is ready to begin rehearsals for a new play, but who has not put any of the actors under contract for the play. Imagine the director getting feedback that the actors wanted their contracts signed, but who states, "Tell them not to worry. I've always been a man of my word."

When an organization changes, some people will have different jobs. Jobs may be anything from almost the same as before the change to radically different. When we want workers to do that different job, we must put them under agreement to do so. And when we need other workers to keep doing their old jobs into the new organization, we need to confirm their agreement to do so. To make things more difficult, we must get folks into new agreements and confirm the old agreement on a one-on-one basis.

Workers in an existing organization are already under agreement to do the existing work. Until we change that agreement with them, workers, consciously or unconsciously, will tend to keep doing what they have been doing. Not only do we need to get workers under agreement for the new job, but we must get them to agree to continue the old job until the moment of changeover to the new one. This step in engineering the performance management system is all about getting a new agreement in place with the workers involved in an organizational change so that they will be willing to perform to expectations. And unlike many other steps in engineering change, the chief change officer cannot do this step. Only an immediate supervisor can get an employee under a new agreement.

Implementation of the VOC cannot occur until each employee is prepared and under agreement for the performance needed. Terms of the contract call on each employee to use the altered processes and PET called for by the VOC. Getting workers under agreement takes careful preparation, systematic execution of a one-on-one contracting session, and after-session follow-up to ensure the agreement for new work can be managed.

Understand What Agreement You Need to Have from Workers

Before meeting with workers on a one-on-one basis, it is critical for the boss to get a clear picture of what he will be trying to accomplish. When this step is completed, we want each worker under agreement to

- perform the needed role in the organization after the change goes into effect to meet specific goals in the new work,
- continue to perform at the needed level for the existing old work job until it is time to formally change the role,
- do the change work transition tasks required to make all the needed mechanical changes to get to the new role (i.e., help in defining the new role and goals, participating in training, work process walk-throughs, etc.), and
- accept the compensation package and title that we will be offering (either changed or unchanged from the present organization).

Get Ready for the Contracting Session

A boss cannot get a worker under a new agreement unless he is under a new agreement himself. Imagine a director trying to get actors under a new contract when the director is not sure she has a job! Getting bosses on board first means that contracting will need to be done in an organizational cascade—from the top of the units affected by the change to the bottom.

The boss must also be ready to explain the vision, the work process and PET alterations that will be needed for that change, and consequently, the role and goal alterations required. Readiness also includes enthusiasm and high expectations for the organizational change. Regardless of the enthusiasm, optimism, and hopes of the change leader in the organization, it is the boss' expectations for the future that count with the employee in the contracting session. Bosses who cannot muster enthusiasm for such sessions with their employees are clearly not under agreement themselves. It is up to each boss to *get* ready, and *be* ready or *go back* to her boss and recontract!

In addition to organizational direction, the boss should be prepared to offer and discuss a compensation package that the worker is likely to accept and the company is able to afford. The boss should have checked with both the change leader and the organization's human resources department to get clear on the compensation package to be offered and whether or not there is negotiating room on any parts of the package.

The materials the boss will need to have in hand for the one-on-one session with his employee include the following:

- The relevant role/job description and job title (frequently the title will be unchanged)
- Statement of individual goals
- Organization chart
- Team assignment
- Compensation package
- Effective date for the organization change

The last and one of the most critical parts of the preparation will be to schedule the worker for the one-on-one session. Schedule a meeting place that will be private during your conversation with the worker, a conversation that could last from 30 minutes to an hour. Be sure to tell the worker that the purpose of the session is to formally invite the worker to be a part of the upcoming organizational change. The worker should already have heard about the change multiple times if you have executed our communication plans as outlined in the first requirement: engineering and communicating vision.

Conduct the Contracting Session to Get Workers under Agreement

The contracting meeting is a business meeting, and it needs to have a planned business agenda. We recommend the following six steps for conducting the contracting session for an organizational change that will require major alteration in what the employee has been doing (for minor changes, the boss can pick and choose how much of the following outline to use):

1. State the purposes of the contracting meeting.
   - Get the employee on board for the upcoming organizational change.
   - Get closure on the role you want the employee to play in the future organization.

2. Describe the organizational change the company has committed itself to make.
   - Explain the VOC.
   - Explain the case for change (why make the change at all and why make it now).
   - Explain how the work in the organization will need to be altered to reach the vision.
   - Explain how the PET will need to change.
   - Explain roles that will need to change to support the work processes.
3. Present the offer to the employee.
   - Describe the role you would like the employee to play in the organization.
   - Describe the level/kinds of goals the employee would have.
   - Describe where the employee would fit in the organization.
   - Present the salary/title change (if any) that would go with the altered role and goals.
   - Discuss the offer with questions and answers.
4. Ask for acceptance of the offer.
   - "We want you to be a part of the organization after the change."
   - "Would you be willing to accept our offer?"
5. Clarify the next steps:
   - effective date of the new organization/role
   - continuation of present job (old work) while organizational change is being prepared
   - participation in the changework needed to assist in preparing for the change
6. Close the meeting with thanks for agreeing to be a part of the change in the organization.

The contracting meeting may go as smooth as silk with the employee readily agreeing and getting on board (usually the case in organizations that have mastered change). Frequently, however, the process is not completed in a 30-minute meeting. The boss may encounter one of the following situations, particularly if the organizational change is perceived as a major one by the employee.

- *The employee needs time to consider.* If that is the case, agree to meet again with the employee after two or three days. Some employees need the time to consider, or they want to check with a spouse. They may even want to get the reaction of other employees who are going through the contracting session.

- *The employee wants to negotiate.* We are offering, in essence, a different job to the employee. Negotiation should not be a surprise and might be looked at as a normal part of a business transaction. The employee needs to be able to consider the new job along with the offered compensation. You must be able to handle the negotiation based on your preparation for the meeting.

- *The employee is unwilling to take the offer.* Some employees may not be willing to take on a new or different role for their own reasons. If so, you might want to be respectful of that decision and do what you can to begin to transition the employee out of the organization before the effective time of organizational change. Having an employee say, "No, thank you," in a contracting session is not necessarily bad news. If this employee would not have been cooperative in the organizational change, it is better that you find out about that in the contracting session and not in the first few weeks of the change when the employee's lack of cooperation could hurt the organization's performance.

- *The employee is not sure.* Some employees may not be sure whether they want to move to an altered position. Some employees may not be able to get rid of their uncertainty until after they are in the altered role. All this is understandable and acceptable to a point. You should not entertain the idea of letting the employee try the new role without getting the employee to agree to a 100 percent effort to do the new role as it needs to be done for a trial period. This agreement to perform at 100 percent is necessary to ensure that the organization can count on the needed performance from that role and so that the employee will really understand and appreciate what the altered role requires and can, therefore, make a better decision about taking the position long term.

Over the years we have had several managers balk at the contracting idea because, as they said, "You are serving up this organizational change as a take-it or leave-it situation!" Our standard response has become: "Yes, it is a take-it or leave-it situation. The organization has decided to make the change. The needed work process alterations and the needed PET are no longer optional. The need for role alterations is no longer optional. The only thing that is optional is whether the employee chooses to work in this part of the new organization." Imagine a contracting session between a director and an actor. When the actor is offered a role in the new play, he says, "No thank you, I like the old play better, and I'll just stick with my part in that play."

Seal the Contracting Session with a Handshake

We shake hands when we buy something. We shake hands when we sell something. We shake hands after a job is offered and accepted. And we shake hands after we have gotten workers to agree to participate in the organizational change. "Let's shake on our new business deal!"

Most companies don't do a good job of changing the agreement with the employee on a one-on-one basis. Companies try to change employee agreements in batch with several employees in the same room listening to a big boss explain what the company needs "from each and every one of you!" That's an important speech to make and I wouldn't do away with it, but I would make sure that the speech is followed by a one-on-one meeting between every affected employee and his or her boss. In that meeting it is up to the boss, representing the employer, to ensure that the employee understands the need for him or her to do the job differently. And it's up to the boss to look into the employee's eyes and confirm agreement to do it the new way and then to consummate the deal with our culture's symbol of agreement—the handshake!

The handshake is the very last act we use to get managers and employees to change to the new direction in the company. The handshake finalizes the renegotiation of an employee's role in the new future of the organization. The handshake represents the employee's intention to perform the new role, as he or she understands it for the accepted compensation package. The handshake represents the company's (and management's) intention to expect and support performance of the new role. Last but not least, the handshake cancels the old role agreement between company and employee.

The handshake, completed under an eyeball-to-eyeball gaze, signals two people's intention to go forward together toward a new way of working. If either party cannot execute the handshake, everybody knows where they are and they can try to resolve the problem of lack of agreement—either through more explanation, negotiation, or by terminating the relationship.

Record the New Agreement

Take that last step and document the organization's records to show that the employee accepted the altered role at the offered or negotiated compensation level. The record should also note whether the acceptance by the employee is for a trial period or the long term. We also recommend that for major organizational changes, the boss pen a letter to the employee thanking him for accepting the altered role in the new organization. Many managers have wished they had such a letter after an employee disavowed any knowledge of the impending change and/or the contracting session with the boss.

TRAIN ALL EMPLOYEES IN THEIR NEW ROLES

 MIND-CLEARING EXAMPLE

Imagine a director who doesn't think the theater company can spare the time for rehearsals. Or imagine the director who says, "All the members of my company are experienced stage professionals. They certainly don't need to go through the humiliation of rehearsing a play in front of an empty theater."

When workers start doing work that is relatively new to them, they need to know what they are doing. How is that for a revolutionary idea? If workers are asked to change to work that they do not know how to do, they will not be able to perform well, and they will probably have bad feelings of fear, uncertainty, and doubt. This step in engineering the performance management system is all about getting the training to workers involved in an organizational change so that they will be able to perform to expectations—theirs and the company's.

Many managers seem to think that training employees for organizational change is no big deal. Actually, we have found a huge amount of confusion around the training that accompanies organizational change. What we want for organization members is the kind of training that theater company members get in their rehearsal for a new play. Employees need training in their roles. Organization members in many of today's organizations have gotten every other kind of training you can think of, without getting any training or rehearsal at all on the roles they are to perform. We have seen the following training courses offered (or made mandatory) to organization members with good intentions of preparing them for an upcoming organizational change:

- The Psychological Theory of Personal Change
- Personality Types and How They Respond to Change
- Stress Management
- Learning Theory
- Creative Thinking and Innovation
- The Theory of the Learning Organization

All the above course titles may be legitimate areas of study, but they don't fit well with an organization that is trying to move from the way it operates now to a new way that has been designed for the future. To make our point, consider the following example. Imagine a director announcing the following training courses to her theater company in lieu of a rehearsal for their new play:

- Theory of the Theater
- Modern Musical Comedy in the American Theater
- The Economics of the Modern Entertainment Business
- Psychological Profiles of Actors with Stage Fright

How would you like to hear what the actors have to say about that? Imagine that their requests for rehearsals of the script are answered with more courses like the ones above instead of intensive focus on the task at hand—learning the ins and outs of the play they will be performing in a matter of days!

Training is important for organizational change, but it must be training that counts toward mastery of the new organizational play that is to be performed.

Get Clear on the Objectives of Training

The objectives of training in the context of organizational change are clear: We want the workers in the organization to be able to do the work that is required for company success because the company will operate in the new way that has been identified in the VOC. We want the workers to be able to do their assigned roles at the needed performance levels, whether their roles are new ones or altered ones. We want to ensure that individuals have the knowledge, skills, and attitudes needed to perform to altered statements of work

We want the kind of training that a theater company gets as it goes through its rehearsals for the new production. Just as we want a cast to run through a dress rehearsal, we want workers to be trained in the roles they will play in work processes after the organizational change.

Arrange the Needed Training

We want to arrange for the training needed for good performance to alter knowledge, skills, and attitudes to the levels necessary after the change. When many managers think about training, they envision the classroom variety of training in which workers hear about the new things they will need to be able to do after organizational changeover. While such classroom training is useful for moving the work force to a level of awareness and preparation for the change, the kind of training that most fills the bill is hands-on practical training. In practical training, the workers get the opportunity to do the required work processes with the required PET on a repetitive basis until they develop the needed level of proficiency.

The kind of arrangements that organizations need to make to execute training needs to vary with the intensity and importance of the organizational change. Obviously, when proficiency in work processes or PET is required for safety or business consequence reasons, training needs to be intensively applied.

- For critical organizational changes requiring high worker proficiency as soon as the organizational change goes into effect, training must be systematic, intense, and repetitively delivered. We watched up close and personal both NASA and the U.S. Air Force training its crews to perform a new mission. And that training is intense, starting months before the new mission commencement date and continuing daily until all crews have the needed levels of proficiency. In such situations, individual crew members receive literally hundreds of hours of training before they get the necessary level of proficiency.
- For organizational changes that only require a minimum level of worker proficiency at the time of the change, training can be applied much less intensively. It is still critical, however, that training brings the work force up to that minimum level before we throw the switch at changeover. We have seen many organizational

changes that involved work process changes with altered computer screens. In many of these changes, the change leaders took the step of arranging some computer training before the changeover and then left the workers to sort out the best use of the software after changeover.

- For organizational changes that require a long trip up the learning curve, training must be carefully arranged to get the work force to the needed level of proficiency within both the schedule and economic constraints of the change. (The learning curve idea has been around since the 1930s and deals with the rate of learning that takes place as workers double the amount of repetition of the job. Industrial engineers can calculate the likely learning rate for the specific operations involved in an organizational change.)

Test to Ensure Readiness to Change

OK, so you can't imagine a director who yells, "show time" before having a full dress rehearsal in which she grades each actor's readiness to go on. Hopefully, you also can't imagine your airline pilot announcing to his expectant passengers: "I'm really excited about this trip. This will be the first time I've flown this baby." For successful organizational change, we want to test each individual to ensure his capability to perform at the needed level.

We have seen organizations where the very use of the word *test* sends off shock waves among the employees. We use the word *test* to mean the same thing that the director does when he views a rehearsal and identifies those actors who need further role development and practice. The rehearsal provides information to the director about what additional coaching and/or repetition he needs to bring to the theater company in transition.

We have also found that it is a good idea to record the training that people have completed and when they pass the proficiency test for the upcoming work. We want to make a permanent record of training and tested performance level. These training records came in handy when we were working with change leaders to understand exactly where they were in a change project they were running or inheriting.

IDENTIFY AND ALTER THE SYSTEM FOR MONITORING PERFORMANCE

 MIND-CLEARING EXAMPLE

Imagine a director who watches a dozen rehearsals of the new play without giving any feedback to the cast. Or imagine a director who schedules a rehearsal but doesn't sit through it. Imagine the director saying after the rehearsal, "I want you to get your feedback from your fellow thespians." Or imagine a director who says, "Let's just wait for the audience to give us feedback on how we are doing. They're the best judges anyway."

When workers start doing work that is relatively new to them, they need to know how well they are doing. If they do not know how they are doing, their performance may suffer because of uncertainty and/or doubt. Or they may conclude that because they are getting no feedback to the contrary, what they are doing must be right on target. This step in engineering the performance management system is all about getting information to workers so that they can feel more comfortable about their work and continue to improve performance.

When workers are in existing jobs for any period of time, they know where they are performancewise because of the measures provided on the job or from routine feedback from customers or fellow employees. When workers are moved to new or different roles, these old ways of getting feedback are disrupted. Therefore, one of the tasks of the change leader is to ensure that there are means put in place for workers in new jobs to understand how well they are doing and what parts of the job they need to do better.

The four most important mechanisms for getting feedback to employees who are new to work are: (1) supervisor input, (2) measurable goals, (3) just-in-time assessment and training, and (4) customer/peer feedback.

    1. *Supervisor Input.* The primary feedback mechanism for new or altered worker performance is the opinion and judgment of the

worker's supervisor. Just as the stage performer looks to the director for signals that she is performing the role as needed in the play, workers look to their bosses to ensure that they are on the right track. If an organization is systematically engineering organizational change, they will have ensured that managers (the bosses) are on board with the change and able to give input to employees who are doing new work. While employees are personally responsible for developing their new roles, we openly encourage bosses involved in change to be aggressive about giving workers feedback. After all, it's the boss' job to direct the play. It is also the boss' job to answer questions. And the more comfortable the boss makes employees feel about the new work situation, the more questions he will get!

2. *Measurable Goals.* Earlier I talked about workers needing performance goals for the new or altered roles they were being asked to play. For goals to be useful in letting people know where they are, measurements must be taken and fed back in a timely manner (real-time is best). It does no good to provide quarterly, even monthly, feedback on progress toward goals. Workers in changed organizations need to know how they are doing on at least a weekly basis.

3. *Just-in-Time Assessment and Training.* Another form of feedback can come from the training resources who have helped workers prepare for the new or altered roles. We recommend that trainers who understand the altered work processes and PET make frequent passes through the workforce to see how they are doing (a very informal role) or to conduct spot assessments or audits of training results (a much more formal role). We have seen organizations put their trainers on call to answer questions from workers in new roles.

4. *Customer/Peer Feedback.* Frequently, workers will get feedback from their peers, either verbally or by watching other members of the organization do similar work. We recommend that supervisors encourage workers to talk to their peers to better understand how things are going, for themselves and others. We have seen companies sponsor lunch meetings of small groups of employees to enable conversation among workers who were coming up to speed on new jobs. Sometimes workers get feedback from their customers on how things are going, although we do not encourage it. We want the workers to know what they are doing without having to ask their customers for a grade.

Before we leave this step, it is important to comment that formal performance appraisal and salary review systems are rarely of value for job feedback during an organizational change. These formal systems are frequently tied to an annual calendar and should be used to give long-term feedback and review to how the employee is doing overall in what might be a string of altered roles. After an organizational change has been in place for some time, the formal systems are of great value for giving feedback about how the worker performed in the past review period.

ALTER AND COMMUNICATE
COMPENSATION PAYOFFS

 MIND-CLEARING EXAMPLE

Imagine an actor who goes on stage for opening night of the new play wearing his old costume and singing his favorite song from the old production. Imagine the director saying, "Well, your performance is not really what I wanted, but here is your paycheck anyway." Or imagine an actor who gets his first paycheck after starting rehearsals for a new play. Imagine the actor complaining to the producer that the amount of the check does not match his newly negotiated compensation and hearing, "We decided not to change paychecks for any of the theater company. That would mean too much work and confusion for our accounting staff."

When workers start doing work that is relatively new to them, they need to see and understand how that new work is related to how they get paid. We all work for pay. Working people follow the money. Money counts. Show them where the money is—and where the money is not—and they will direct themselves toward the money and away from the deficit. The challenge for the change leader is to compensate employees for the work that matches the VOC, and to not compensate for work that does not align with that vision.

The two compensation principles that apply in engineering organizational change are:

1. Compensation is earned when performance, as defined in the new, altered role, is delivered at the level agreed to in the agreement with the boss.
2. Continued performance of the old role will not result in any compensation from the firm.

We have found no more difficult job than convincing change leaders and managers that they must pay for the employee work they need, and not pay for the work they do not need. While this sounds simple enough, it is very difficult to get managers in some companies to act in this emotion-laden area of performance management.

The need to match pay and performance is sometimes easier to envision in the case of vendors or contract employees. No capable manager would pay contract employees for doing old work that was no longer a part of the statement of work in the vendor contract. (Imagine defending yourself to your boss if you did.) And no capable manager would go forward with new vendor contracts and then refuse to pay except under the terms of the old contract.

Unfortunately, it is very common after changeover to see change leaders and managers paying workers their regular salaries even though the workers have not yet adopted their new roles in the changed organization. Paying workers even though they do not change their roles sends an immediate signal to these workers and those around them that working in accordance with the vision is not required or desired. So there are actions that need to be taken to ensure the compensation system pays off for change and doesn't pay off for failure to change. These steps involve mechanically changing the payoff rules in the company's performance management system and then following the rules for compensation with a great deal of discipline.

Align the Payoff Rules with the New and Altered Roles

The idea of payoff rules is simple. We want to have a set of rules or guidelines that tell us what to pay and when to pay it for different performance levels. For a vendor, we have terms in the contract that state that the payoff will occur after certain specified work has been satisfactorily completed. The specified work is normally listed right in the contract so there is no confusion about what work goes with what pay. In some vendor contracts, we find incentive compensation—extra dollars that the vendor might receive if the work is done in some exceptional way. Normally, the criteria for determining the extra inventive compensation are listed in detail.

For employees, such payoff rules are more often implied than written into an explicit contract between worker and employing organization. The payoff rule normally followed by a company is that the worker is due an agreed upon monthly compensation when the work called for in the job (as documented sometimes in a job description) has been satisfactorily performed. In some companies that offer incentive compensation, additional dollars might be won by the employee by achieving certain goals or targets. Many companies write down these targets at the beginning of the target period (usually a year) so they can make any incentive compensation calculations needed at the end of the year after work results are available for evaluation.

The change leader's job is to replace the old job description that drives salary with the new job description of the altered role. In addition, the change leader must ensure that all old goals in the files or paperwork have been replaced by the new ones that go with the altered roles.

This is not rocket science, but it is engineering and the details count. If we have 30 workers moving to altered roles and goals, somebody needs to ensure that there are 30 altered job descriptions and sets of goals inserted in the company's files in place of 30 old role descriptions and goal sets. This paperwork change is absolutely necessary so that the company's accountants—who ensure that everyone in the company gets the right check at the right time—can do that accurately.

Follow the Payoff Rules
on a Day-to-Day Basis

Changing the paperwork is a key first step to ensuring that the organization will pay for the performance it wants and not pay for performance it does not want. But the critical ingredient that makes the pay for performance linkage work is the boss. Which boss? Every boss! Every boss in the organization must follow the payoff rules to the letter to ensure that employees all align their behavior with the vision. Every boss must:

- *Coach workers toward performance on the mark.* The boss' job is to ensure that the workers on his watch are moving toward peak performance in altered roles—working altered processes using altered PET—to achieve the VOC. The boss' goal should be to win for the company while coaching each employee in how to win as well.

- *Give real-time feedback for performance off the mark.* When a boss sees performance off the mark (not aligned with the vision), she should give real-time feedback to the worker to give him the chance to get back on track. More coaching might be required to show the worker how to do that or to get the worker's skills to the desired level.

- *Provide counseling for performance off the mark.* For workers whose performance is repeatedly off the mark, the boss should provide counseling, exploring with the employee the reasons why performance does not comply with the direction in the vision, or coaching. The goal would be to assist the worker in the steps needed to get back on track or to consider leaving the organization or role.

- *Put jobs at risk for those employees consistently off the mark.* If a worker is not willing to perform to the mark, the boss has no choice but to tell the employee that his employment is at risk. That is, the boss says, "You have not demonstrated the kind or level of performance this organization is willing to pay for, therefore we are putting you on probation." Most companies already have a policy or procedure for dealing with unsatisfactory performance. In situations like this, the boss should work directly with her human resources department to ensure that her intentions and needs are within the organization's guidelines.

- *Remove employees who don't comply.* Organizations that want to master change to deal with today's turbulent business environment must be willing to take firm action. Failure to remove someone from the organization who refuses to go along with an organizational change can send a message to other workers that will cripple the organization's future change capability. Our experience is that one removal in an organization is a powerful message that organizational change is truly not optional.

8

Engineering Action Plans for Change Work

The fifth requirement of engineering organizational change is to construct and fully communicate action plans and schedules for change work for each week or month of the transition to the new work. Action plans and schedules detailing the week-by-week change work that must be completed to get to the vision are needed by workers who must know what change work to do on Monday morning, along with the old work they are already doing.

For a minor organizational change, the amount of change work to be done may be quite small, involving only a few workers or work processes. But for a major organizational change that will involve many workers (maybe thousands) and several work processes (maybe dozens), the amount of change work that must be completed can be huge and overwhelming.

Manage Change Like a Project

I have used the word *project* several times in this book, but not with the degree of emphasis needed for mastering change. I mean to treat change work as a real project that has an identity as well as a manager with the authority and resources needed to get it finished. I mean that change work must be managed with the discipline of project management—a specialized and well-developed management field that deals with getting unique work done in an organized, systematic, and timely manner. In Chapter 6, I talked about the discipline of construction management, a form of project management, and how that was essential to the alteration of PET. In this chapter on the engineering of action plans, I unabashedly state that change work must be subjected to disciplined management. And the closest developed capability to what is needed here is project management.

Leadership for the Change Project

If change work must be managed like a project and special attention must be given to the management of all the risks, who is the project manager? The project manager is the official, formal, organization chart leader of the organization that is making the change. Only the big boss has the final authority to put an organizational change into effect.

Imagine a director telling the investors in his new play that he decided not to be responsible or accountable for the preparation of that new play. Imagine the investors' reactions when he says, "I really hate all this preparation stuff. I'm going to let my assistants be responsible for it."

While the boss cannot escape the ultimate accountability for organizational change and for the management of the change project, he can use able assistants to help. These assistants can be most helpful if they have project management and/or construction management skills. In fact, starting a big organizational change effort without an experienced project/construction management professional in a key support role is an almost certain recipe for a change that will come in off target, off schedule, and way over budget. It is still interesting to us as consultants to see managers who would not dare tackle the construction of a major capital asset without a pro-level construction manager, but not think twice about tackling a multimillion-dollar organizational change without an experienced project management professional.

If a project management professional is to be added to the change project, the following skills and experiences are critical to success:

- Knowledge of the company and industry
- Broad organizational knowledge
- Strong project planning and scheduling skills
- Flexibility and versatility
- Excellent interpersonal and communication skills
- Negotiation skills
- Information technology capability for scheduling and communication

This chapter is all about getting in control of the needed change work so that the desired organizational change can be made—on target, on time, and on budget. Getting change work under control requires a project management mindset, a robust planning and scheduling method that includes a master schedule and timetable, critical path planning, work breakdowns, weekly schedules, and several one-on-one meetings with the workers involved in the change. And as a critical overlay, getting change work under control means explicit and disciplined risk management.

A critical discipline within project management is the management of risks to the project. Taking an organization that is doing old work and changing that organization to new work is not an easy or certain exercise. The size of these risks can be anything from a few thousand dollars for small organizational changes to hundreds of millions for potential disruption to a large organization or to its customers. There are many risks along the way, risks that must be explicitly and aggressively managed for the change to be successfully completed.

We have identified three categories of risks that must be managed during the process of organizational change:

1. *Technical risk.* This is the chance that various parts of the change will not work the way they were planned. Technical failure could be needed equipment that does not work as intended, work processes that do not achieve the desired result, and so on. (Imagine

the props in a new theater production functioning so poorly that attention was diverted away from the actors.)

2. *Organizational risk.* This is the chance the organization will not accept the change to the new work. While some folks might say that the biggest obstacle to acceptance is work force resistance, we would say that the biggest cause is failure to meet the requirements of engineering organizational change. Imagine actors on the stage for a new performance who clearly do not have their hearts into the play.

3. *Business risk.* This is the chance the costly-to-implement organizational change will not pay off in dollars and cents for the implementing company. Failure to gain a business outcome could be caused by a number of factors, from poor design of the change (presenting a new way of working that customers do not like) to flawed implementation (causing even a good organizational change design to feel wrong to customers and employees alike). Imagine a new performance of a musical comedy that is well executed by the cast but that just isn't funny.

We doubt that there is an experienced worker anywhere who has not seen an organizational change that either did not work (from a technical point of view), was not used, or made no money for the organization.

Organizations vary significantly in their capabilities to manage risk. In today's modern organizations, we frequently find a well-developed risk management function that can be very helpful with some technical aspects of an organizational change. Usually the strength that we find is associated with the organization's PET and is focused on the management of technical risk. Whether an organization is installing a new piece of factory equipment or a new software application, the odds are that the installation will be successful and the new PET will work as advertised (or at least close to it). The best layman's definition of the technical risk is associated with the critical questions: Will the PET work? Will it work on time? And will it come in on budget? This kind of technical risk, while occasionally mismanaged, is usually handled quite well by a combination of the company's professionals and its vendors.

A well-conceived organizational change can promise and deliver important business results in today's highly competitive business environment. But delivery of those results is highly dependent on disciplined risk management that handles all three major risk categories: (1) technical risks, (2) organizational risks, and (3) business risks. Unfortunately, that kind of comprehensive risk management is a tall order for many of today's organizations that generally focus on technical issue resolution alone while organizational and business risks are left to chance. The organizational change message is very clear: Plan to manage all three kinds of risks effectively or keep what you have in the way of old work. Moving ahead toward new work without managing all three risks is a certain recipe for organizational disruption and even disaster.

SET AND COMMUNICATE THE MASTER SCHEDULE FOR CHANGE WORK

 MIND-CLEARING EXAMPLE

Imagine a director who has no master schedule for the work to be done to transition her theater company from the old play to the new one. When asked about the calendar dates for key transition events, she answers, "Well the situation is much too fluid to put things down on a calendar. We'll just have to wait to see how things play out, won't we?"

In the first four requirements for engineering organizational change, we have identified much of the change work that will need to be done:

- We have a vision that needs to be detailed and communicated to the organization.
- We have work process alterations that need to be made.
- We have alterations to make in PET.
- We have individual worker role alterations to make and contracting sessions to conduct.

The trick is to look at all the needed change work as a project. The project must be managed to get the needed change work done in an organized and systematic way while the organization carries on with its old work. The single most important tool for getting the needed change work done is the master schedule.

The master schedule has its place in the overall timetable and sequence of activities associated with organizational change. While that place may vary, companies that have mastered change put the master schedule as the first step and use it to guide change leadership all the way from vision development to the changeover to new work. The general sequence of change activity follows these nine steps:

1. *Development and communication of the master schedule.* The change leader sketches the beginning and desired end points of the organizational change and creates the high-level master schedule.

2. *Development of the vision and the case for organizational change.* The change leader launches those activities needed to develop in some detail the VOC (the new work to be done by the organization) as well as the case for change.

3. *Initial communication of the vision and case for change.* The change leader begins the communication process designed to give the organization a heads up to changes that are to be made along with the reasons for those changes.

4. *Identification of change work.* The change leader names teams to identify needed alterations in
   • work processes,
   • PET, and
   • performance system (i.e., worker roles, training, etc.).

5. *Development and communication of a detailed master schedule.* A detailed master schedule is created to show the calendar for completing all needed change work.

6. *Alteration of worker roles.* The change leader authorizes bosses to conduct one-on-one contracting with workers for
   • starting new work at changeover,
   • continuing old work, and
   • conducting change work.

7. *Conducting and verifying all change work.* The change leader ensures all the needed work gets done, including alteration of work processes, PET, and roles, and then tests to ensure that all needed alterations have been adequately made.

8. *Changing over to new work.* At specific times the various parts of the organization make the switch from old to new work.

9. *Break-in or learning curve phase.* The change leader aggressively leads during the first few months of new work, during which the organization continues to learn and make further refinements to work processes, PET, and worker roles.

Critical Attributes of the Master Schedule

Regardless of the magnitude of the organizational change, the master schedule should have the following attributes to be a sound base for engineering change:

- *Comprehensiveness.* The master schedule must include all parts of the organizational change, not just the most visible parts (like the purchase and installation/modification of PET). Work process and role alterations, contracting sessions, and training classes all go on the master schedule.
- *Realism.* We have seen timetables for organizational change that are about as unrealistic as driving your SUV to the moon. Change work takes time and energy and must fit into or around the already busy schedules of the workers. Realistic time estimates for completing the different kinds of change work must be developed and then combined if the change is to have any chance of being completed on target, on time, and on budget.
- *Business fit.* As we have said before, organizations do change work while they continue to do old work. Scheduling change work must take the schedule of old work into account if the schedule is to be realistic. For example, scheduling work process alterations for an accounting organization while they are in the thick of preparing tax returns for a April 15 deadline is courting schedule disaster. On the other hand, the master schedule must also take into account the realities of the needed change. If the organization must have a change done by a certain date to maintain its level of profitability, that reality must be dealt with in the schedule.
- *Critical path schedule.* This kind of schedule shows what change work must be done in what order so that all the change work has the most time-efficient flow to it. For example, imagine trying to train employees on new equipment that has not yet arrived. The critical path method is a key discipline within project/construction management and is an absolute requirement for projects that have more than a handful of change work steps. Computer-aided project management tools usually include critical path planning capability.

When we finish explaining master scheduling to our change management clients, we frequently hear, "Oh no. Do we really have to do all this detailed planning and scheduling work?" The simple answer is,

"Only if you want to have a chance of completing your organizational change on target, on time, and on budget." As I have said before, change management is not rocket science but it is engineering— disciplined, detailed hard work. And using a detailed master schedule is a requirement of engineering organizational change.

Setting the Master Schedule

Building a master schedule these days starts with the selection of the project management software that will be used to schedule and manage the project. If you are using a skilled project manager, odds are she already has experience in such project management packages. You may also be able to count on your organization's information technology department to provide you with the needed software package and maybe even somebody to run it for you.

The high-level master schedule can be developed around the change sequence shown earlier in this chapter. The detailed master schedule can be completed after the change leader has a feel for the needed alterations. Input for developing the master schedule can come directly from the alteration lists discussed during the four earlier requirements for engineering change:

1. The VOC (the detailed version as described in Chapter 4)
2. Process alterations needed to reach the VOC (as described in Chapter 5)
3. PET alterations needed to reach the VOC (as described in Chapter 6)
4. Role alterations needed to reach the VOC (as described in Chapter 7)

While a project management assistant might be able to make the first pass at getting these lists of needed alterations into the project management software, it is the responsibility of the project manager to sit down with that list of activities and turn it into a schedule. We have found this task to work better if the project manager and her assistant also have the time and energy of some of the people who produced the lists of project alterations. Their input will be invaluable in identifying the two critical parameters needed for a critical path schedule: (1) the sequence of alterations, and (2) the estimated time to make alterations.

Odds are that multiple rounds of scheduling might need to occur before the change leader settles on the master schedule she wants to communicate. For example, one round of scheduling might be made using the desired target for changeover to the new work. This will need to be done first if the change leader has named a desired time frame during the development of the VOC. This step frequently shows that "you can't get there from here," as the old saying goes, meaning that all the needed change work may not be possible before the desired new work date.

The second round of scheduling might start with the current date to calculate the projected finish of the change effort. The outcome of this round gives direct feedback on the realism of the original desired changeover date. The change leader can rework the scheduling process as needed, adjusting time estimates where possible to get a master schedule she can live with.

Communicating the Master Schedule

The change leader must communicate the master schedule to the key managers of the organization who must be cognizant of the change so that they are prepared to lead their department's share of the change work and to shift to the new work at the targeted changeover date. Because the master schedule will contain a lot of detail (given, of course, the magnitude of the change), all of the organization's managers don't need to see it all. They just need the parts that involve them and their units.

The only practical means for communicating the master schedule to the managers in an already-busy organization is with a face-to-face meeting with them. Until then, the master schedule is just another e-mail attachment or floating piece of paper.

The change leader must also create the conditions under which the master schedule will be heard as official notification of actions that must be taken by the involved managers in the organization. If organization members see the master schedule as for your information only (FYI) or nice-to-know information, they clearly will not be positioned to contribute to an organizational change—on target, on time, and on budget.

Developing the Change Budget

Organizations that have mastered change cannot only bring in a change on target and on time, but on budget as well. The logical exercise that goes on alongside the master scheduling process is project costing. Experienced change leaders know that changing an organization takes real money out of pocket just like building a house takes money. The elements of an organizational change that cost the most money are frequently associated with alterations or new PET. However, other alterations also take money. Listed below are some of those parts of a major organizational change that generate costs for the project budget.

- Alteration of PET, including costs of engineering and construction, vendors and the disposition costs of old PET.
- Alteration of work processes and writing procedures requiring overtime or professional services fees.
- Alteration of worker roles, including training costs, new uniforms, possible salary adjustments, etc.
- Development of the vision, frequently requiring professional fees for consultants, market research, benchmarking, etc.
- Addition of extra personnel to work the change, including contract programmers for development/modification and project management of software applications, and/or change management specialists to support the work of the change leader and the organization's managers.

The idea is to get to a sound estimate of the cost of organizational change by estimating the costs of the pieces of organizational change. We have used two different approaches that work reasonably well for getting at the costs of organizational change. The first approach is called the proposal approach. In this approach, the change leaders ask that specific effort and cost proposals be prepared for each identified part of the organizational change as it is planned. Over time, an organization can build up a history of change project costs that will be useful for such proposals.

The second approach is called the business plan approach. It calls for the change leader to look at the organizational change as the start-up of a new business. Business people who have approached a bank about a loan for a new business quickly find out that they need a pretty thorough business plan to convince the banker that their dollars will be well invested. A convincing business plan shows the structure of the desired new business, the vision, and the revenues that can be expected. In addition, the plan must show all the important moving parts that will ensure the vision is reached. The business plan will need to identify all the actions and assets needed to reach the vision and the total costs that will be required. We have asked numerous clients to prepare a business plan for change as a part of change management. Results have varied from consistently good business plans from some companies to mediocre plans from others. One clear positive result of requiring the business plan, however, is that the requirement forces the changing organization into a mindset that explicitly recognizes the financial cost of change.

Beyond these two approaches, we do have one last resort method to use in the absence of any organized change budgeting. We usually recommend the simple rule of thumb: determine the costs of the new or altered PET, and at least double that figure to get an order of the magnitude of the total costs that will be incurred in the change project.

Few companies today will launch a major capital expenditure project without a time schedule or cost budget, but it is quite common for organizations to undertake a major organizational change with neither, except for those parts of the change that involve a construction project for some of the visible PET. Organizations that want to master change must treat scheduling and budgeting for change just as seriously as they treat budgets and schedules for the normal work of the organization, such as making and selling products/services for a profit.

USE WEEK/MONTH-AT-A-TIME IMPLEMENTATION SCHEDULING

 MIND-CLEARING EXAMPLE

Imagine a director who is transitioning his theater company while continuing to perform the old play. Imagine the director using a detailed daily schedule of performances for the old play (specific days and times for each performance, days when there will be cast substitutions, etc.) while using only a high-level schedule for transition to the new play, showing only what months will be devoted to costume fittings and rehearsals.

This step is a simple but an often-neglected one. While managers in the organization that is changing need a master schedule to understand what they must do and when they must do it, their workers don't need a detailed schedule of the entire project. The workers do need an overall time frame for making the organizational change. But what they need more is a time schedule that fits their normal work routines. If the old work of their organization is scheduled on a once-a-week basis, change work schedules need to be served up on a once-a-week schedule as well.

If we want workers to continue to do their assigned work in producing products and services while doing change work, we must help them by providing both lead times and scheduling of change work that allows them to make the inevitable adjustments that must be made during times of change. Failure to keep workers informed of change activities has been the downfall of many changing organizations. There are few things that hurt worker morale more than having them surprised by elements of the organizational change. The kinds of surprises that we have seen while doing our change management consulting range from the simple, inconsequential surprise, to what appear to be life-changing surprises:

- Surprise relocations of the department, including worker desks and on-the-spot moves to another plant.
- Disconnection of phone and/or computer lines without warning to workers.
- Changes in signage renaming departments or work processes.
- Impromptu training classes that workers do not know they have to attend or have no time to attend given their other work responsibilities.
- Unexpected arrival of new equipment or tools, or departure of old equipment and tools.

Our goal is to have each worker see the change work that will be needed in time to get it done along with the old work still being done on a day-to-day basis. For each week/month of the implementation, we want to show those communication and alteration tasks to be accomplished. Keeping well-planned and well-followed schedules for change work in front of workers on a week-to-week or month-to-month basis not only keeps workers informed, but it pays extra benefits as well.

- It says to workers that change work is a regular part of our business along with old work.
- It says to workers that the organization cares enough about them to keep them informed about what is happening in the place where they work.

- It shows orderly progress toward a targeted changeover to new work while letting the workers know that the organization is really serious about change.

Make One-on-One Implementation Assignments

 MIND-CLEARING EXAMPLE

> Imagine a director who schedules all of the actors in his company to show up for a costume fitting at the same time when the seamstress can only handle the one-hour fittings of one actor at a time. Imagine the director saying, "Well, I can't do everything for you. Surely you can handle a little scheduling problem."

So, where are we? We have developed a VOC and communicated that vision across the organization with particular emphasis on the parts of the organization most affected by the intended change. We have identified all the alterations that will need to be made in the organization's work processes and PET. We have identified the individuals who will be impacted by the change, and we have determined the role alterations that will need to be made by those folks to be in sync with the new work. We have already had an important one-on-one conversation with each affected employee to get him or her under agreement to perform the needed new work after changeover, to continue old work until changeover, and to perform the needed change work to get ready for changeover.

This step is designed to ensure that each worker involved in an organizational change knows exactly what change work needs to be done literally every day until changeover. We recommend that managers use one-on-one meetings with each employee affected by an impending change to officially launch the change work that will need to be done by the employee. This one-on-one meeting reaffirms that we have the worker under agreement to do the change work.

We have found that change work gets kicked off much better with much greater likelihood of results when there has been a face-to-face conversation between manager and employee about upcoming events such as training classes, office moves, and familiarization sessions on new equipment. Merely posting a change schedule on a bulletin board near affected workers will not get them launched on the path to change.

After the one-on-one conversation about change work, workers may continue to address change work as needed with the assistance of a weekly schedule. But more one-on-one conversations will need to be held during scheduled change work to ensure that the worker has the support, direction, and resources necessary to get the change work done along with old work.

We must keep the workers' situation in clear perspective to ensure that we can support this critical step in engineering organizational change. It is critical to keep in mind that workers in the midst of change are like the theater company members who are called on to perform the old play every evening while they spend parts of the day getting ready for the new play. During this critical phase of completing change work, workers still have responsibility for completing old work during the time periods when they will also be attending training classes, executing office moves, and so on. It falls to the manager of those workers to provide the support needed to be able to accomplish two critical things at once. Managers can arrange to have other workers cover for those workers who are in training classes, arranging for temporary employees to do some of the old work—or the change work for that matter—such as executing parts of office moves.

This one-on-one meeting step calls for some big shifts in what many managers do on a daily basis. It is quite common for managers in a smoothly running organization doing old work to have very infrequent contact with workers. After all, everybody knows what to do and how to do it and everybody is going about business as usual. When it is time for change work to get done in an orderly and systematic way, it is critical that the manager change the frequency of contact with workers. Bottom line, we want to ensure that each individual who has a task to do in implementation of a change has a clear assignment and responsibility for doing that work and has the day-by-day support of the supervisor in getting that work done.

REGULARLY CHECK PROGRESS AND RESCHEDULE

 MIND-CLEARING EXAMPLE

Imagine a director who sets a schedule for the transition period to the new play, but never checks the schedule. When asked by the producer how the transition is going, the director says, "Oh I gave you a schedule a couple of months ago when we started the transition."

"Never a horse that ain't been rode, never a cowboy who ain't been throwed." And never a change effort that goes just the way it is planned. Change leaders can count on many things about the organizational change to go differently than planned. This fact does not in any way lessen the need for good planning and scheduling. Good plans and schedules are the best tools for dealing with the inevitable interruptions, diversions, and obstacles that appear in the path of every organizational change. Organizations that have mastered change expect the unexpected, continually monitor for implications for the change initiative, aggressively reschedule change work to keep the overall change initiative on track, and clearly and quickly recommunicate modified schedules.

Expect the Unexpected

The change leader can count on several of the following situations to occur on his watch:

- Shifts in market demand for the organization's goods and services.
- Turnover of key members of the organization.
- Problems with key customers (they change a big order, cancel a big order, make a fuss about delivery of that order, and so on).
- Competitive challenges, like the introduction of competitive products or decreases in competitor prices.
- Interruption of critical supplies to the organization.
- Introduction of new regulations.

In addition to the situations above, the change leader can expect there to be surprises in the change work itself:

- Equipment installation takes longer and costs more than planned.
- Equipment gets installed but doesn't work the way it was intended.
- Training sessions do not enable employees to achieve the needed level of proficiency.
- Workers change their minds about moving to new work.
- Communication glitches foster confusion and misunderstanding.
- Leaders change (key task force members or project schedulers leave the organization or transfer to a part of the organization that is not involved in the change, and so on).

When these inevitable situations occur, the change leader must face two realities. First, these situations must be satisfactorily handled. And, second, the organizational change initiative must continue movement toward the change—on target, on time, and on budget. There are, of course, some situations that occur that might cause the change initiative to be canceled, but those are usually rare. Now is the time for the change leader to hold the fort and show the flag.

Monitor for Implications of Change Work

Imagine a director who was so engrossed in preparation for his company's new play that he did not notice major problems in the night-to-night performance of the old play. Closer to reality for most of us, imagine the change leader who is so intent on making the organizational change on target, on time, and on budget that she does not see what is happening to the old work of the organization. The change leader must be focused on both the running of today's business (because that's what pays the current bills for the organization) and the changing of the organization (because that's what will pay the bills in the future).

As each day goes by, the change leader must identify those situations which might impact her change effort and determine the potential implications of those situations. The two major kinds of implications that we want to watch for are:

1. *Obstacles to change work.* These are situations that will require an organizational response that will in some way interrupt the important actions on the master schedule and/or the change budget (i.e., a crises erupts with an important customer that

requires most of the personnel in a department to drop everything and rescue the situation, during the very week the department personnel were to be trained on new work processes).

2. *Issues with the design of the change.* Issues here are of two
   kinds. First, as the change begins to unfold, flaws may be found
   in the design of the vision itself. It may be that the potential value
   of the vision may not prove to be as great as once envisioned. In
   that case, the vision may need to be altered, requiring modifications in the change work to be done. Second, the business environment outside the organization might change impacting the
   potential effectiveness of the vision. Once again, the vision may
   require modification.

Reschedule to Keep Momentum

The two main drivers of the rescheduling process are (1) the interruptions and obstacles that we have just discussed, and (2) what the organization has learned during the change process. As the change work
unfolds in the organization, some parts of the change are likely to go
better than expected. For example, we could learn that training a department in the new work processes takes only half as long as expected. Or
we might learn that the installation of PET costs less and/or occurs
faster than originally planned. Any of the things learned during the
change might be used to produce a reschedule that is more effective
and/or more efficient. Managers who have mastered change expect to
learn things during a change and are prepared to take advantage of them
quickly in the reschedule and rebudget process.

There are two approaches to the reschedule process that we have
learned to use simultaneously.

1. *Schedule extension approach.* The first approach is to treat all
   schedule changes as alterations to the last and most current
   schedule. In this first approach, we are keeping the logic and
   sequence of the very first scheduling process in play as we identify needed schedule alterations called for by interruptions and
   obstacles.

2. *Zero-based scheduling approach.* The second approach is like
   the familiar zero-based budgeting concept and calls for us to
   periodically rethink the overall logic and rationale of the entire
   master schedule. We stimulate this kind of thinking with questions like: If we were setting our master schedule today for the

first time, what general order and logic would we use? Given what we know today about the organizational situation, how would we lay out the change work needed before changeover?

The use of both these mindsets or approaches produces the best overall way to look at rescheduling. The most difficult change management environment our firm has ever worked in required rethinking the change work schedule every Monday morning to take into account unfolding events of the previous week. Not every change situation will be as complex as this engagement, but regularly rethinking the schedule has proven to be a critical skill for our consultants.

Most rescheduling efforts will be driven by the simple need to go around logistical obstacles. But sometimes we will find the clear need to alter the logic or sequence in the change schedule. The change leader must always keep in mind that he is doing two things at once: (1) supporting the organization as it continues to do old work getting out its products and services to today's customers, and (2) keeping change momentum in place for an organizational change that is on target, on time, and on budget.

Quickly Communicate New Schedules

When reschedules are necessary, and they will be necessary, it is important to quickly and clearly communicate the new schedules to those organization members who need them. If you have assigned qualified project managers to assist in change leadership, they will be versed in requirements of competent scheduling and rescheduling. They will have established guidelines for keeping track of schedules to ensure that the organization always has the current schedule. Obviously in big complicated change projects with many moving parts, just keeping track of who has what schedule can become a big job. Clearly the current movement toward Web-based project management and scheduling can be a major tool for ensuring both currency and availability of good schedules.

CONFIRM AND CELEBRATE THE COMPLETED CHANGE WORK

 MIND-CLEARING EXAMPLE

Imagine a director who hears through the grapevine that transition work has been done, but never goes or sends anyone to check to make sure. Imagine the director at a pre-opening night party toasting the company, "If it's not done by now, we'll find out after the curtain goes up tomorrow night."

Old-time managers who have "been there and done that" tell us to "expect what you inspect." Such trite phrases have lost much of their popularity in an era of participative management and flat organizations, but show me a theater director who will move confidently to opening night without multiple dress rehearsals. Show me a producer who feels confident to face investors with the words of the director who says, "Aw, we don't need full dress rehearsals. They just waste valuable time and put wear and tear on the set and costumes."

This confirmation step is designed to test the organization's final readiness to execute the changeover to new work. It is also about finding those last remaining trouble spots that must be ironed out before the organizational change can be made—on target, on time, and on budget. This step is one more opportunity to show the flag supporting the change that is about happen for the company's betterment.

Make Sure that Alterations Have Really Been Made

The truth of the matter in change management is that the organization is not ready for change until it is ready, and a changeover should not start without confirming that needed alterations in work processes, PET, and employee agreements have been completed. The message here is simple: double check to make sure. But the change leader's goal in this confirmation step should be to come across as a leader, not just an inspector.

Check and confirm that change work has been done in the following areas:

- *Work processes.* Look at process diagrams for the new work; look for new procedures; see if you can find the old procedure manuals that are marked for destruction after the changeover date.
- *PET.* Look at newly installed PET; view equipment tests; look for new operating guidelines; and view the plans for taking old equipment out of play after changeover.
- *Performance management.* Interview employees; ask them to tell you about the new roles they will be performing; ask them to walk through the new work processes they will be performing; check their understanding of the changeover date.

Completion of these confirmation steps will provide some confirmations of change and some confirmations of problems. Once problems are identified, then the master schedule must be modified to reflect those actions that will be needed to complete change work.

Confirming readiness for changeover also includes checking for currency. For some of the mechanical properties of organizations, the saying "once changed, always changed" just does not apply. For example, training records might reflect that training has been completed, but employees may not be current. Training workers too far in advance of the changeover to new work will usually be wasted because none of us retains new knowledge or skill without putting it to use.

Celebrate Successful
Completion of Change Work

So why do theater folks hold those preview performances followed by cocktails for the theater company and selected members of the specially invited audience? Preview performances accomplish a number of things that the change leader also needs to accomplish:

- *Final check on readiness.* Preview performances serve as additional dress rehearsals used to hone the theater company's readiness.
- *Ending of change work.* Preview performances are confirmation with the cast that preparation is ending and new work is about to start, symbolically moving to the performance stage.

- *Thanks for change work.* Preview performances show appreciation for the hard work of preparation. "We recognize and value your hard work."
- *Commitment.* Preview performances are the last confirmation of full commitment of each and every member of the company to the new play.

Organizations cannot hold a preview performance as easily as a theater company, but they can do something to get many of the effects of one. We recommend to our change management clients that they hold a celebration near the time of the changeover to symbolically confirm readiness and commitment. Such a celebration also says thank you to workers who have been getting ready for the change. We want the celebration to add energy, enthusiasm, and momentum to the individuals, teams, and units involved in the implementation of change.

PART FIVE

Managing Change

Organizational change is a journey that does not occur in a vacuum. Organizations change what they are doing while continuing to produce today's goods and services at a profit. The manager's job in change is to make it possible to get to the desired future in an organized and efficient way that accommodates the change capacity of the organization and its members.

9

Running the Business While Changing the Business

 MIND-CLEARING EXAMPLE

Imagine a theater company's director with a vision of no lost performance days in transitioning from an old play to a new one (i.e., the Saturday night audience will see the last performance of the old play and the Sunday matinee crowd will see the first performance of the new play). Imagine this director frequently talking about the new play, but focusing solely on the nightly performance of the old play with no time and thought given to the work that obviously must go on during the day for the transition to the new play. After each tiring performance of the old play, the director instructs the company to go home and go to bed: "Let's just sleep on what we've got to do to transition to the new play. We'll see you here again for tomorrow night's performance."

DOING TWO THINGS AT ONCE

An important client of ours recently replied to my innocent question in a way that knocked me sideways. I asked him to tell me his single biggest challenge. His answer came back like a shot: "I feel like I've got to run this business every day or we're not gonna eat at the end of the month. And I feel like I've got to be changing the way we do business or we're not gonna be eating this time next year!" So there it was, right out in the open—the thing that many managers struggle with the most and the thing that many consultants don't seem to get at all—the absolute, inviolate need to change an organization while it is operating.

THE REQUIREMENT TO RUN
AND CHANGE AT THE SAME TIME

In earlier parts of this book I talked about requirements associated with changing the mechanical attributes of the organization. Now we see another requirement. Today's business leaders are required to run the business while changing the business. The leader of today's organization must do what the director of a theater company must do when he is required to run the old play until Saturday night and open the new play on Sunday afternoon. This director cannot shut off the old performance and declare a 90-day preparation period for the new play—and neither can the business leader who faces an organizational change. In both cases, the show must go on!

In addition, business leaders must do as good a job changing the business as they are doing running it. And today's business leaders are, for the most part, doing very well running day-to-day business. In fact they are doing such great jobs running the business that a less-than-great job of changing the business stands out like a sore thumb. Today's requirement to run the business in an excellent manner (or be beaten to death in the competitive marketplace) generates still another requirement.

In many companies, however, leaders report they are not doing a good job of changing the business. During our training course "Run the Business/Change the Business," we always ask participants to help us with a little unscientific poll. We ask participants to use a one-to-seven (bad to good) scale to rate how well their company is running and changing the business. Invariably the scores come back in the five-to-

---

FIGURE 9.1 Adopt the Dual Perspective

Rule 1: Adopt the Dual Perspective

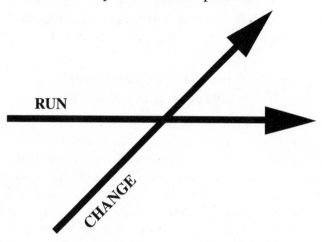

---

six range for running the business and the two-to-three range for changing the business. We then ask if the low score for changing the business is a problem and the answer from the audience is yes.

This chapter is going to be all about doing two things at once—and doing them both well. We'll go beyond theory to the practical tools many of our clients use to see, describe, and effectively manage the two apparently conflicting initiatives of running the business and changing the business. We will cover these practical tools as a set of simple, even familiar, rules that most managers will be able to understand and follow in a flash. You will learn how to use many familiar management tools in a slightly new way to change the business.

RULE 1:
EVERYONE MUST HAVE
THE DUAL PERSPECTIVE

The starting point for running the business while changing the business is maintaining what we call the dual perspective. We illustrate the dual perspective with the crossed arrows in Figure 9.1. The horizontal arrow pointing to the right represents the running of our day-to-day business, fulfilling today's orders for today's customers using the means the company has at hand. The diagonal arrow pointing to the upper right represents the initiatives we are taking to change the way we are currently doing business—changing work processes, modifying PET to match those changed processes, changing employee contracts, and providing necessary training to perform the new processes.

Keep the Run-and-Change Mindset in Daily Business

Adopting the dual perspective means that everyone in the organization must keep both directions in mind as they do their daily business. Some of our clients have immediately argued that the dual perspective is too tough a concept for workers. We have definitely not found that to be the case. We have only found a handful of workers in the last five years who could not understand the common sense notion that if we don't run the business today, we won't eat at the end of this month; and if we don't change the way we run our business to make it better, the competitor down the street will try to make sure that we don't eat this time next year. Another silly idea we have encountered is that workers can't keep both mindsets going at once. Nonsense. Those of us in the work force are quite capable of walking and chewing gum at the same time. And we can clearly think about doing work today and how we are going to change the way we do that work tomorrow.

Getting the Dual Perspective across the Organization

Understanding the dual perspective is one thing; getting everybody to accept it as their job is another. Unfortunately, most employees in many companies were hired during a time when change was the exception and not the rule. When many of these folks were hired, they heard (or somehow concluded) that their job was only to run the business (that is, to do the same kind of work over and over again with little change). Then, many of these workers kept the same job for years without much change. Regardless of how some workers gained a run-the-business mindset, that condition must change. With change as the rule and not the exception, it makes no sense to have workers on board who are not signed up for both running and changing the business.

Getting the dual perspective in place across the organization will require a change in the performance contract. Leaders who want to be successful at both running and changing the business must have everyone in the organization under agreement to participate and be accountable for both. To complete this new agreement, senior managers must go first, demonstrating with their own behavior a focus on both doing today's business and working today to change the way business is done. Then leaders must talk openly and often about change being the rule and about the new agreement the company needs to have with all employees. Follow-up, one-on-one conversations will be needed with everyone in the organization. These one-on-ones can be conducted with each employee at normal performance appraisal/salary review time and/or whenever an individual encounters a specific change in his or her job situation.

Just as the leader of a theater company must always be thinking about both the current production and the next one, so today's business leaders must be continually using the dual perspective. And just to make sure we have clarity, it is no longer possible for any manager in the company to hold a job with only a run-the-business mindset.

RULE 2:
POWER BOTH PERSPECTIVES

We take as self-evident that organizations need continuous energy from leadership or those organizations will tend to lose focus on either the run or change fronts. We are not making a case against empowerment of workers. We are simply observing that the organization members we call leaders are normally held accountable to ensure that the organization stays focused on desired results, and that the means to get those results are working properly and are adequately resourced. Our way of thinking calls for leadership energy to power both the run-the-business and the change-the-business perspectives.

Separate Leadership for Running
and Changing the Business

Not only must there be energy to power both perspectives, the energy needs to come from different sets of leaders, as illustrated in Figure 9.2. For us to have a chance of success at change, we must

---

FIGURE 9.2 Power Both Perspectives

Rule 2: Power Both Perspectives

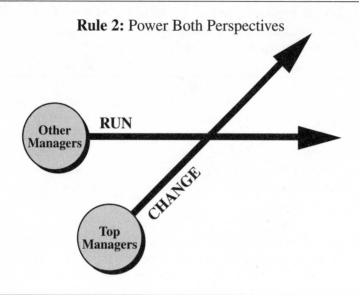

---

depend on top management to supply the leadership energy and focus necessary to power the change-the-business perspective. Managers other than top management supply the leadership energy and focus necessary to run the business. While we are saying that only top management should lead change, and only other management (the cadre of managers) should lead the running of the business, we are not saying that these two groups should operate separately. Both top management and other management are involved in changing the business, but top management leads. Both top management and other management are involved in running the business, but other management is in the lead.

This leadership distinction is critical because usually only top management has the authority, credibility, and organizational horsepower needed to effectively lead change initiatives. We have seen many change efforts fail because there was not enough top management horsepower applied to a change. Everybody in almost all organizations is busy for most every hour of every day. We need leaders who can get our attention and pull us out of the trees to see the forest. In addition, we need leaders who insist that we will both run the present business and do our part to change the business. And we need someone to tell us that, not because we are blind and dumb, but because we are busy. Top management must be in that change leadership role for change to succeed.

FIGURE 9.3 The Wrong Energy Sources for Change

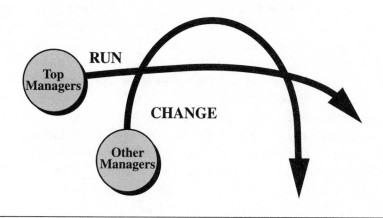

The Wrong Energy Sources for Change

Many companies try to change with the wrong leaders powering change. Figure 9.3 shows what will happen—sooner, rather than later—if senior management focuses on running the business while changing the business is left to other managers. With senior managers focused on running the business, the organization is likely to decline over time because needed energy is not being applied to changing the organization to stay competitive. Sure, other managers are trying to lead and focus the change-the-business initiatives, but they are not likely to be successful if top management is running the business because their top priority emphasizes today's products for today's customers. Not only will the organization suffer from this misplaced use of energy, but the other managers who try to make the change happen will frequently become the victims of fatigue, burnout, and sometimes political damage. Leadership distributed like that shown in Figure 9.3 just doesn't work, and everybody who has been in an organizational change knows it.

Imagine the leader of the theater company and his senior people (including the stars of the old play) continuing to focus on nightly performance of the current play while the less senior folks and the stand-ins head the transition, set the tone, and arrange the needed changes for the new production.

Directing Senior Management
to Change Leadership

Why don't organizations always focus their top management on change? We have heard a number of reasons for wrongly configuring leadership for change. First, there is the logic that says because many companies have not had to change that much (or that often) in past decades, many top managers today made it to the top by being hands-on, day-to-day runners of the business. In short, many of these leaders may be running the business because it's what they know how to do, it's what they do best, it's what they want to do, it's known—while changing the business is unknown. If this is the reason for top management to focus on running the business, we suggest the following: "Get over it. Focus your talents and energy on the change side or you will lose that top management position and any security you had with it."

Second, we hear top managers say that they are needed to run the business because business is so difficult today. "The other managers in the firm can't run the business as well," they say. "They don't have the knowledge or the experience or even the temperament for it." And we have seen this to be the case in some situations. Top management's first move in getting ready to run and change the business at the same time is to fix the management shortage—and quickly. There are organizations that are so thinly staffed that there are few managers left other than top management to run the business. In these cases, it's up to top management to figure out a way to get itself extracted from day-to-day leadership by any means available. We have seen top managers delegate to lower level managers more than they wanted to, creating self-managed teams at the worker level and doing whatever it took to off-load run-the-business daily leadership to give themselves time to focus on change.

But the most common reason top management gives for why other managers can't handle run the business is that top management has not done its job of building an organization with the talented people needed for today's environment of change. In many cases, we have a clear case of a self-fulfilling prophecy around the running of the business: we don't believe other managers can do it, so we don't let them do it, so they never learn, and sure enough, they can't do it. Today's organization must have talent other than top management necessary to run the business on a daily basis or the organization will have no chance to stay up with the competition.

FIGURE 9.4 Guide Change with a Clear Vision

Rule 3: Guide Change with a Clear Vision

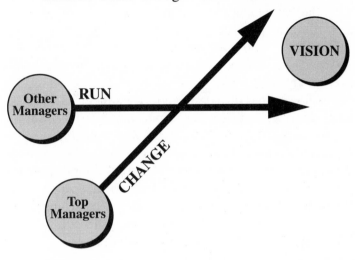

RULE 3:
GUIDE CHANGE WITH
A CLEAR VISION

For employees to be able to meet their run-the-business and change-the-business responsibilities they must have a clear and understandable picture of the desired organizational future—the vision for organizational change.

Rule 3 calls for us to keep our vision of the organization's future in clear sight while we both run and change the business. This means that all the managers in an organization need to have a clear idea of where we are taking the organization so that they can ensure that their day-to-day actions in running the business do not compromise the eventual destination, and so that the day-to-day changing of the business will have the right general direction, as illustrated in Figure 9.4.

Craft a Change Vision

Before I launch into a big discussion, let me remind you that we did a real number on the idea of vision in Chapters 3 and 4. At this point in our discussion, we just need to make a few simple points about the kind of vision that is needed to guide an organizational change while we are running our day-to-day business.

We must craft a vision that will drive change. A VOC must show future run-the-business results that obviously cannot be achieved without significant changes in the way the organization currently does business. It must provide the case for change. If the vision does not make the need for change obvious, it cannot serve as the needed direction or energizer for change.

Besides showing our final destination, we want the vision to be clear and detailed enough so that it can become the basis for the day-to-day change initiatives called for in Rule 3. Some of the biggest problems that we have encountered in change have to do with what we call the wrong kind of vision. For a vision to be useful in guiding change, it needs to take on more of the characteristics of the theater company's script. Rather than a good half page of bullet points listing the desired attributes of the organization's future, we may need full pages of details describing how the future organization will need to look to be successful.

Just to make sure we are clear on the idea of a detailed vision, consider the following example from the theater. Imagine a director who tells the theater company about a new play using only the following list of attributes. "The new play will

- be a world-class musical comedy,
- be filled with contemporary dance numbers,
- have engaging music, with one or two key songs for popular sale,
- have a unique quality to the *whole* of the production, and
- have actors who express their individuality through their passion for their roles."

These attributes could describe any number of Broadway shows, but the point is simple. The above list is not adequate information to lead a cast that knows nothing about the future performance to a winning production of *Cats*. To be useful for guiding change, the vision we paint for an organization must have enough meat to it to allow the employees to understand what the organization will need to look like in the future and the changes that will need to be made to the current organization to get to the new one.

Besides giving direction for the change, we want the vision to bring some sense of stability to the organization during the change. As an organization moves from one state to another, things can get very confusing, particularly at the detailed level. We want the employees to be able to look to the organization's vision to get a sense of orientation about just where they are going and why some of the detailed steps might be necessary.

Keep the Vision Communicated and Up to Date

For the vision to be useful, it must be visible to the organization at all times. For employees to get it, to see it as their real future, the vision will need to be communicated frequently and openly—almost to a point of sensory overload. We want the organization to be saturated with the vision as much as a director wants the actors to read and reread their new script and rehearse every day.

For the vision to be credible, it must be kept up to date. If our view of the future changes or if our desires change, a new or updated vision is called for. Somehow we have gotten a message to many managers that a vision, once detailed, cannot be easily changed or the organization will become disoriented. We have found in practical experience, however, that the exact opposite is true. The organization knows when its vision is out of sync with some new marketplace reality and they read "out of sync" as "leaders asleep at the switch." So when the vision needs to change, change it. Keep it fresh and up to date. Show the organization a leadership team that is with it and on the ball, and you're more likely to have an organization that's on board.

RULE 4:
LEAD WITH TWO CLEAR AGENDAS

Lead the organization with two agendas—one for running the business, the other for changing the business. By *agendas* we mean goal or project lists. As shown in Figure 9.5, if we want the organization to have the dual perspective and to change the business while running the business, we must provide clear goals and project lists for both perspectives. We can easily imagine the theater director with two separate lists that both must be worked—a list of *to dos* for running tonight's performance of the old play and another list showing those things that must be done before opening night of the new production.

FIGURE 9.5 Lead with Two Clear Agendas

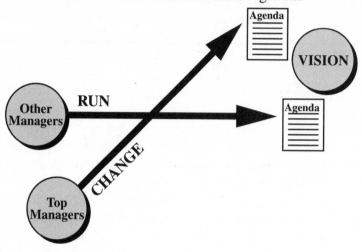

Rule 4: Lead with Two Clear Agendas

Almost all organizations have a list of the things they want to accomplish. We call it their run-the-business agenda; they call it their profit plan, their budget, or their list of company goals. Most businesses develop a run-the-business agenda on an annual basis. It's usually a big deal exercise for the company to assess where they are at the end of a year's operation and to identify targets/goals/budgets for the next year. This annual exercise is taken very seriously. Managers know that the best tool for giving their organization a sense of direction for the upcoming year is a clear, concise list of goals.

The Need for Specific Agendas

If it makes sense to have a clear set of goals for the running of the business, doesn't it also make sense to have a clear set for the changing of the business? Ask managers this question and they are likely to tell you, "Of course it does." But in the real world of organizations that are trying to change, we rarely find one that is clear about its change goals for any given year. We frequently find a changing company with a relatively clear profit plan for the coming year, but a too-general vision of the future and only a fuzzy idea of what needs to be done by somebody in the coming year to get the organization moving toward change.

Experienced managers know that a clear set of specific objectives will win the attention of employees over a set of fuzzy, generalized, rambling instructions every time. Give employees the choice of accomplishing specific goals or of following a fuzzy trail and they will almost always put their attention toward the specifics. Why? Because most employees know that what they receive from the organization is somehow linked to what they get done and it's easier to show progress on the specific list than on the generalized one.

The point is simple: if you want the organization to both run and change, you better have equally clear sets of goals and objectives for the running and the changing of the business. And we stress the words *equally clear* for the two lists. Our experience is that the goal lists that are the most clear and specific are the ones that will draw the most attention.

If the point is so simple, why do many companies not have a clear, concise set of change goals for a time period? We're not sure why so many don't, but the hypotheses abound in our office. Maybe it's because of the difficulty of translating a vision into specific actions that need to be accomplished. After all, the present business probably took decades of design and improvement to look like it does now. For the change agenda items, we are asking management to design an entirely new company in some respects. No wonder it is difficult.

Maybe companies don't have change agenda items because they haven't thought about the need for specific goals for change the same way they have for running the business. For many of us, change has always been the exception and not the rule. Regardless of the reason, there is no excuse for not having a list of crisp and clear change goals. Without such a list, an organization's chances of getting to its vision in any kind of organized and logical way are slim.

Developing the Agendas

So two lists are called for. Where do we get them? The goals on the run-the-business agenda come out of the company's normal profit or business planning cycle. In this cycle, company planners forecast the business/market situation, competitor moves and positions, general economic conditions, and many other things to come up with ideas for next year's goals. These goals are normally expressed in terms of what we call operating results—sales revenue, market share, customer satisfaction, position on industry indices, return on investment, and so on.

Normally the list of goals is short. Some experts recommend no more that seven goals for any one list.

The process for identifying goals for the changing of the business is very different, but not all that complicated. When a company establishes its vision for the future, it puts in place the foundation needed to derive its specific change goals. Change goals for any given year come from the long list of steps the company will need to take in order to reach its future vision. We call this long list of steps the *change queue*.

In short, a company can list all the steps (or changes) that must occur in its operating attributes or assets—its image, products, processes, technologies, plants and equipment, employees, and the way they behave—in order to become the future vision. Then for each calendar year on the way to that vision, the organization's top management selects a handful of the steps that make the most sense to accomplish in the upcoming period in order to progress toward the vision. The criteria for selecting items for a given year's change agenda should be based on: which steps need to get done in what sequence and which steps make sense to do given the nature of the run-the-business work we will likely do next year. This isn't rocket science, as the following example shows.

A company in the business of servicing energy production had been focused for more than a decade on the North American market. The company had considerable success with its services and decided that the future for them lay in expanding services into the three other large production markets: the Middle East, the Far East, and the North Sea. After thinking through its vision in some detail, it came up with a number of change goals for the coming year, including the opening of an office for sales and service in the Far East. It chose the Far East because its activity forecast showed the best chance of new business in that part of the world. For this company, the number one item on its change agenda for the new year was to open a sales/service office in the Far East. One of the company's vice presidents was promptly assigned the responsibility for this key step.

Run and Change Goals Are Different

This simple example does help to make some clear distinctions between run and change goals. While run goals are normally stated as results, change goals are stated much more like projects or initiatives. Change goals are frequently those actions or steps that will need to be completed for the company to achieve its future vision.

Another distinction between the two types of goals has to do with permanence on the agendas. While a company may have a market share goal on its run agenda every year (changing the exact target number as needed given the forecast), a change goal may not be seen again once it has been accomplished. In the above example, once the company had opened its Far East office, the item disappeared from the change agenda and was replaced by a different change goal.

Some care must be taken when selecting change goals to ensure that progress can be made. In the above example, opening the Far East office was chosen because it was clear, relatively simple, easy to measure, and doable in a relatively short period of time. Accomplishment of the change goal would not have enabled the company to get all the way to its vision, but the opening of the office was an important, concrete step along the way. Had the company chosen a goal of getting some Far East business in the new year, whoever had the assignment might have spent time making sales calls rather than putting in place an important, concrete step the company would need to reach its vision.

For change goals that are really tough or long range, we recommend breaking the goals into shorter-range, intermediate milestones whose accomplishments will show some progress and keep the organization's momentum going.

The Need for Short and Sweet Agendas

Change agendas need to be kept relatively short and sweet to have any chance of drawing and focusing organizational energy. We have all seen far too many companies with change lists that were so long and so comprehensive that the company became overwhelmed. And the net result in all these cases has been too few results. We would rather see an organization accomplish four important items on a change agenda than see 20 change goals that are not well met.

Now before you accuse us of totally missing the complexity and reality of big organizational change, let me offer more detail. As I write this chapter, our company is working with two oil companies that are merging their downstream assets into a single refining, transportation, and marketing organization. The new organization, a joint venture, will be about the fortieth largest company in the U.S. with annual sales of more than $20 billion. Its change agenda for 1998 had only three simple things on it: (1) complete and sign the joint venture agreement, (2) merge the physical assets into one system, and (3) harvest several million dollars of synergies. Three key items were on the top line of the change agenda, but underneath, the change project manager was working with a critical path diagram containing more than 2000 detailed steps.

Whether a company has three big items on its change agenda or more than a thousand change objectives down at the detailed level, we believe that each change goal that is well met can be an immediate source of organizational energy for the journey to the vision. Energy and increasing momentum can result if the change agenda and results are regularly communicated to the organization. In most companies today, there is a confusing array of task forces and committees working on change that causes many employees to scratch their heads because they see no pattern or unifying target. We have found that showing the change agenda with its list of change projects (with an organizational chart of the assigned task forces and committees) can clear up much of the confusion.

And what happens when a change goal is met? It is replaced with another change goal that must be accomplished to reach the destination. The change agenda becomes what we call the running hot projects list that is back-filled continuously and never runs short of work to be done.

The bottom line on these two agendas is simple and straightforward. If we really want the organization to run and change at the same time, two equivalent agendas must be put in place. For the company to put emphasis on both running and changing the business, the lists must be equally specific and relatively short telling the organization that these two short lists are the highest priority things the company needs to get done in the next period. While all managers in the organization are involved in both agendas, top management leads the accomplishment of the change agenda while other management leads the run agenda.

Perhaps the biggest payoff of the idea of the change agenda is that it takes a relatively complex task—reaching the vision—and turns it into a list of straightforward steps to accomplish for the next business period. As we tell our clients in change, "Just make sure you achieve those change goals and the vision will take care of itself."

FIGURE 9.6 Establish Scorecards and Consequences

Rule 5: Establish Scorecards and Consequences

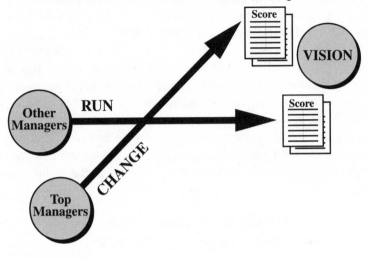

RULE 5:
ESTABLISH SCORECARDS
AND CONSEQUENCES

This rule is no surprise. If a company has a list of important run-the-business goals, it will probably have a way of measuring the accomplishment of those goals. In addition, key managers in the company will likely be assigned the responsibility for goal accomplishment, and their compensation will likely be tied to results. Why do it this way? Because managers have learned over the long haul that assigning responsibility, measuring results, and tying compensation to those results really works.

Measurement, Accountability, and Consequences for Results

If a company expects results on its change agenda, the same rules should apply. Each item on the change agenda must have a measure. Someone must be held accountable for results on that item, and somebody's compensation must be tied to the result. It's that simple. If we want results on both agendas, we must manage those agendas in the same way. Figure 9.6 shows that we must measure results of both agendas and tie results to personal compensation.

For whatever reason, many companies try to change without giving the same weight to change-the-business goals as to run-the-business goals. We rarely find a company that doesn't tie run-the-business results to the compensation of its key managers. At the same time, it is relatively rare to find a company that gives the same accountability and compensation weight to results on the change agenda. In many companies, we see management compensation tied solely to run-the-business results. When managers from these companies ask why their change plans are not working, we have a very simple answer, "You may be saying *change* with your words, but you are saying *no change* with your dollars." Guess which message will be read as the real message?

Visible Scorecards for Both
Run and Change Agendas

The idea of a scorecard for viewing results has been receiving more attention lately. We have found that scorecards that are visible to the organization are very helpful in communicating what is important to the company and showing the progress the organization is making. Seeing positive results go up on the scorecard gives the organization some excitement and momentum. And seeing unwanted results helps put the pressure on and creates the needed sense of urgency to get things fixed.

In the change-while-running situation, scorecards should reflect both run and change results and reflect these results in a relatively equal manner. If run results are recorded monthly, change results should be shown monthly as well. As the organization processes the continuing stream of change results, there will be a much clearer picture and recognition of the change that is being constructed right before its eyes.

So what might appear on a change scorecard? The change scorecard is simply a progress report on the milestones associated with items on the change agenda. In the earlier example of an energy service company placing an office in the Far East, a scorecard entry might be something as simple as "Office Location City Determined—Singapore" or "Lease Signed for 5000 Sq. Feet of Office at 312 Avenue of Asia

Blvd." We want the scorecard to reflect actual results that show real progress on constructing or positioning the assets that will support the vision being implemented.

We can extend this simple example to the run scorecard. Because the service company's vision calls for it to sell services in three markets outside of North America, the run scorecard might be modified by adding scoring slots for sales in all four markets. Three of those scorecard slots will remain empty (or show zero dollars) until the selling assets are in place and the company starts doing business in those markets. But the added slots on the scorecard convey a very clear message: this company is going to do its thing in four markets.

In today's world where change is the rule and not the exception, we want people to know that organizations are serious about change. We want them to know that their job is to both run and change the business. This knowledge will not come easily unless people are held accountable and compensated for their performance on both fronts.

RULE 6:
MANAGE RESULTS IN
TWO FORUMS

Astute managers know that it's a good idea to get the troops together on a regular basis to assess how things are going and to talk about the future. We believe that having such get-togethers to assess results is absolutely critical, especially when you are trying to change the business while running the business. In fact, we have found it important to get together around both run results and change results. It's easy to see the theater director having two different meetings—one that focuses on readiness for tonight's performance of the old play and another meeting focused on those actions that need to be taken to get the new production ready for opening night.

The Importance of Management Forums

Our recommended way of assessing results is through what we call a management forum. By a *forum* we mean a regular meeting of managers who are responsible for the results of the company. In the meeting, we expect to hear those managers who are accountable for results give reports on progress and the next steps for their assigned goals or areas. Then we expect to hear discussion around the table as the man-

---

FIGURE 9.7 Manage Results in Two Forums

Rule 6: Manage Results in Two Forums

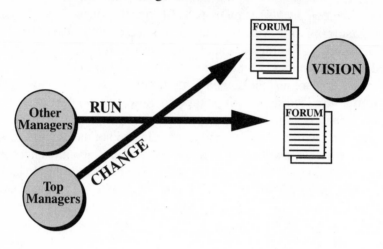

---

agers assess the reported results compared to expectations. The discussion usually ends with agreed upon next steps for the reported item—next steps that may range from "keep up the good work" to "we need to go back to the drawing board." Of course, the worst thing the reporting manager might hear is the reassignment of the goal or project to someone else.

Most well-run companies already use management forums for their run-the-business results (we have heard these meetings called everything from profit meetings to variance reports). Some companies have monthly meetings while others opt for quarterly reviews of results.

We feel that it is critical to review change results in a management forum as well. The organization must focus the same management energy and intensity on change results as it does on the run results. However, we have found that an effective review of change results cannot happen inside a forum in which run-the-business results are being discussed.

Separate Forums Keep the Dual Focus

As illustrated in Figure 9.7, we feel that it is critical to have a separate change forum for discussion of change results. Yes, we are suggesting an extra meeting that is exclusively focused on change. Just what you need—another meeting! An organization that is both running and changing is doing two important things at once. And each of these important things calls for concentrated management attention and teamwork. Two meetings it is. Read it and weep.

We have had multiple clients try to cover both result areas in the same meeting with equally bad outcomes. Run results always take the priority and the lion's share of the time in a forum designed to discuss both result areas. The typical outcome is that change gets the short end of the stick, sending a message to those present that change is not important.

The Need for Equal Forums

Not only should the run and change forums be separate, they should be equal in order to send the dual perspective message. If the run-the-business forum is held in the boardroom, the change-the-business forum should be held there as well. If the format for the run forum is formal (with colored slides and laser pointer), the format for the change forum should be formal as well.

These equal forums really are a big deal, particularly if the company trying to better manage its change is one that has been using what we call the change retreat approach. Some companies, it seems, are only comfortable talking about needed changes during an offsite, management retreat (frequently with super-casual dress, interspersed work and play sessions, and, of course, the hired gun facilitator). Our complaint is really not about the offsite idea: we hold many such meetings. Our point is that the offsite cannot be the sole place to work on change. If it is the sole place for dialog about change, the organization will pick up an old and erroneous message that change is the exception and not the rule or that change is not a part of the regular way this organization operates.

Do offsite meetings to your heart's content, but keep the meetings balanced. Cover both run and change topics. And when you get back to your regular work area, cover both topics just like they really are equally important in the way you do your business.

Bias the Separate but Equal Forums

Each forum should be biased toward its targeted result, but have cognizance of the other agenda. For example, in a run-the-business forum, we expect that the results reported will be operational (from business unit profit, to orders shipped, to inventory level and costs to date). In the discussion of actions that might be needed to get back on track in an operating area, the managers in the forum should be aware of the impact of those considered actions on the change agenda. The forum must ensure that the run actions it approves don't take all the steam out of the change agenda. It frequently takes strong leadership from senior management to keep things balanced here because it's frequently an easy out to take energy away from change to get an immediate run-the-business result.

The discussion in a change-the-business forum should be focused on those initiatives or projects that are aimed at meeting change goals. But we don't want blind pursuit of change initiatives in the face of potential problems, nor do we want conflicts with the run-the-business agenda. The goal is to work the change initiatives in an integrated fashion, trying as much as possible to allow the company to get both kinds of results. In short, these two separate but equal forums will have to be run with considerable wisdom and lots of give and take to make both run and change successful.

RULE 7:
LEAD CHANGE THROUGH
OPPORTUNITIES

In a way, the six rules I have identified so far are all oriented to what we call positioning the organization to be able to change the business while we run the business. The first six rules in essence put the management and organizational machinery in place to get both jobs done. Rule 7 focuses on the day-to-day operation of the business and gives very specific guidance for how to meld run-the-business work with change-the-business work.

Tie Change to the
Running of the Business

In our experience, the companies that have mastered change do a very good job of tying their run-the-business work directly to their change-the-business work. That is, they know how to tie a change initiative to a key run-the-business initiative so that two things get done at the same time.

In our very simple energy company example, we have a company that wants to do business in a number of new markets including the Far East. It has on its change agenda the opening of a new office in that part of the world. What if the company had the opportunity to support an existing client by doing some work in the Far East such as work that called for personnel from the energy company to staff a six-month project in Singapore? This opportune situation might provide the chance to get an office opened in Singapore while performing a key run-the-business initiative that will make money for the company.

This point is one that you might have been concerned about. If we want a company to pursue several items on its run agenda and also on its change agenda, aren't we just adding more work for the company to do? The simple answer is yes. It is a lot more work to run and change a business than it is to simply run a business. We are adding real work that takes real time and real resources and uses the same people to do both jobs. What we want to do is to take every opportunity to combine run and change work to decrease what is already more than a full load for many of today's organizations.

Flex the Change Agenda
around the Run Agenda

We want to take every opportunity to tie an item from our change agenda to a real-time, important run-the-business item. In fact, we may even disregard or remove an item from our change agenda in order to substitute one from our change-initiative queue that fits better with the run-the-business goals.

That is in fact what happened with the energy company we have been following. Its big order came not from the Far East but from the Middle East while it was in the process of looking for an office site in the Far East. This company handled the challenge with a huge dose of common sense. It scrapped its plans for a Far East office in that business year and instead opened its first outside–North America office in the Middle East. It made the swap to take advantage of the resources that were being mobilized for the big Middle East order and to tie to senior management's travel requirements. It opened its first office with plenty of management involvement and attention. The company opened an office in Singapore a year later.

Companies that we have seen handle change the best are willing to be flexible with their change agenda initiatives. They are willing to let the run-the-business initiatives lead because they are what is keeping them in immediate sync with their customers and investors. As in the energy company example, it was flexible enough to take advantage of run-the-business opportunities as ways to work its two agendas at the same time.

Flexing the change agenda was easily done by the energy company in our example. But things aren't always that easy in every company. In some companies, once something gets on a list and somebody's name gets tied to it, the list seems to become a stone tablet. In these cases, it's up to senior management to take the steps necessary to remove a change initiative from the agenda and put it back in the change queue. It's senior management's job to show that changing a stone tablet can be an important act of innovation—not failure.

When we emphasize the connection of change initiatives with run-the-business opportunities, we are using the idea of opportunities in a larger sense. To us, an opportunity could be a new order from an existing customer, a larger-than-normal order, or a big problem with a customer. *Opportunity* means a business transaction that has some special attribute that will allow us to tie it to change. Opportunities normally get the attention of top management.

Keep Senior Managers in the Lead

Opportunities provide the chances for top management to get in on the situation to ensure that both the run side and the change side get worked. We worked with the president of an aerospace company who was famous for personally getting into a run-the-business situation and leading it from start to finish. The not-so-perceptive observer might have seen a senior executive involved in leading work that was a couple of levels too low in the organization to merit such attention. The more perceptive observer might have noted that when the president took over a project, say a large order to be worked through the manufacturing plant, he caused that order to be worked in ways that forever changed the company's work processes. He was a master at running the business while changing the business. And he did the run/change thing totally implicitly. His gut led him to the right order for his involvement and to the changes that needed to be made in the way orders were handled to meet the needs of the future.

For those of us not quite so intuitive, we suggest four actions, illustrated in Figure 9.8, for management to take to ensure that both run and change business are being done as effectively and efficiently as possi-

---

FIGURE 9.8　Lead Change through Opportunities

Rule 7: Lead Change through Opportunities

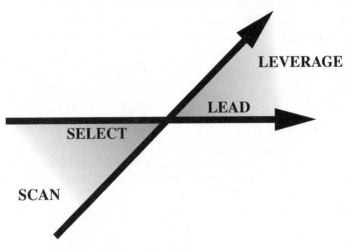

---

ble. First, we want senior management to continuously *scan* the run-the-business situation to look for opportunities—business transactions that might be carriers of change initiatives. Second, we think it is important for senior management to *select* those run-the-business initiatives that are both critical for next year's business success and that could be potential carriers of change initiatives. Selection means to pair an initiative from the change agenda with a key run-the-business transaction. This takes some courage to do because our intuition might lead us in the opposite direction. We are suggesting putting it all on the line by working a change as a part of a key run transaction (changing a major work process while we complete the biggest order of the year).

Third, senior management's job then is to personally *lead* what are now the selected paired or joint initiatives for both the running and the changing of the business. We believe that it is critical for the senior manager to communicate to the organization the importance of the joint initiatives and the reason for personal involvement at the senior level. In situations like this, there is little room for failure of either part of the joint transaction. But with success comes the fourth action—the chance to *leverage* the good results. There is no better role model for running while changing the business than the senior manager who personally shows how it is done.

The Need for Guts and Determination

Running the business while changing the business takes a huge quantity of guts and determination. It took real guts and resolve for the president of the aerospace company to tie a major change of manufacturing processes to the single most important aircraft order of the year. It was clearly a big job to gear up for the new order. It took his fanatical determination to change the work processes at the same time. That's the kind of leadership it takes to run and change and there is no substitute. Gutsy, dedicated leadership following the seven rules can get real results in running the business while changing the business.

This chapter has been all about doing two things at once—and doing them both well. We focused on the practical tools (or rules) many of our clients use to see, describe, and manage effectively the two apparently conflicting initiatives of running the business and changing the business.

We wouldn't be surprised if this chapter hasn't also produced another result. After seeing the ideas in this chapter for the first time, many managers tell us that they now more fully understand why many of the change efforts in their organizations have failed. Well, better late than never. Next time you have a change (and there will be a next time), you will be better prepared to get change results and for running the business while changing the business.

10

Managing Change Realistically for Company and Employees

While the amount of needed change may be great and the time short, the organization can only accommodate so much change before it bogs down. At the root of this change capacity problem lie the attributes of human beings. While we are immensely adaptable—capable of juggling several balls at once and able to survive ambiguity—we human beings have physical limits. It is the role of the change leader to control the rate of change so that it *maximizes* the employees' and the organization's change capacity, without overloading it. In addition, organizations develop an identity over time that limits to a large degree what they might become.

TODAY'S CHANGE ENVIRONMENT

 MIND-CLEARING EXAMPLE

Imagine the director of a theater company who comes to each night's performance of the old play with all the ticket sales numbers of the dozen or so other theater companies staging plays nearby. Imagine that director fretting out loud about whether or not he should change the company's newly selected play to one that has more of the attributes of the nearby plays. Imagine this director adjusting his theme for the newly announced play on a day-by-day basis as he hears how the other guys are doing.

Today's organizations live in a fast changing business environment. Companies face changes in customers, products, markets, competition, technology, communication, regulation (or deregulation), company/work force size, worker attitudes, and, above all, economics. An alert chief executive can easily spot changes in the business environment that might pose threats to or opportunities for his company. But it is up to that executive to cautiously select which and how many opportunities or issues merit an organizational response.

Figure 10.1 is a chart we frequently use with our clients in change management to make key points about managing organizational changes. The figure shows four different change environments ranging from Environment A (long periods of time with no organizational change followed by a change and then another long period of no change) to Environment D (continuous organizational change over a long period of time). We frequently ask our clients to tell us about the four environments. Their response frequently sounds like this: *A* is what we can barely remember, *B* and *C* are what we have been encountering the last few years, and *D* feels like what is happening to us right now. In fact we even have one client CEO who refers to Environment D as *white water* which he says the organization can look forward to in the foreseeable future.

The job of the chief executive is to manage as many changes as needed, up to but not exceeding the organization's capability limits. Our experience as change consultants suggests that organizations have

---

FIGURE 10.1 Possible Organizational Change Environments

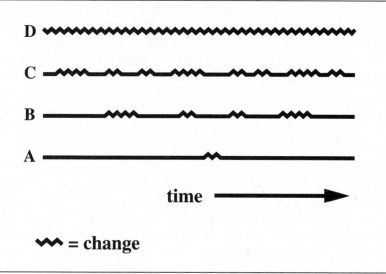

---

in fact moved from the relatively rare change requirement (change is the exception, not the rule) to environments with more frequent changes (change is the rule, not the exception). But we have not seen an organization that is successful when there is always a change effort going on that affects everybody. While the business environment may feel like white water to the chief executive, it is his job to ensure that the organization does not encounter constant change. It is his job to control the change throttle by selecting some business issues and opportunities to respond to while ignoring others.

UNDERSTANDING ORGANIZATIONAL CAPACITY TO CHANGE

Organizations have a finite capacity to deal with change. Capacity limits are determined by both the psychological capacities of human beings and by the identity that an organization develops over time. When viewed together, these two limiting factors pose a real management challenge during periods of organizational change.

Limits Posed by the Capacities of People

During these times of frequent and relentless change, it is vital to remember that some critical things have not changed and, furthermore, will not change. These critical, nonchanging things are the God-given attributes of human beings. While the organizational environment changes at an increasingly quicker pace, the way people attack work hasn't changed. World economics may be turning topsy-turvy at warp speeds, but Mother Nature has not seen fit to change our four basic, work-critical attributes: (1) focus, (2) order, (3) tolerance for uncertainty, and (4) stamina.

As mature human beings, we have been gifted with the ability to focus on several things at one time. Most adults, for example, can handle seven digit phone numbers quite well. (That may be why we have seven digit phone numbers.) Most of us can handle three or four projects at one time by alternating our attention from one to another. But Mother Nature built in some real limits to our marvelous capacity. Move the phone number to 10 or 13 digits, and watch people scramble for a piece of paper and pencil to write it down. Put people on 10 projects rather than four or five and watch overall productivity and performance go south.

We work better with lists of things to do if we can see an order in the list or have some sense of priority for the things we need to do first. Our need for order and priority is so strong that we will create our own priority if it is not otherwise available. We create that order by evaluating each item on the list with a personal algorithm such as, "what's in it for me?" or "what's easiest to get done?" If we can't find our own priority, and if none is available by any other means, our overall motivation and ability to attack the to-do list diminishes, sometimes to the point of complete shutdown.

Most people react to uncertainty in predictable ways. Complete certainty about situations is not motivating; for many of us, it's actually boring. A small-to-moderate amount of uncertainty about work or a job situation may actually excite us a bit, make us curious, or pull us into the game. But high levels of uncertainty usually hit us very hard. While some of us have a high tolerance for ambiguity, most of us are confounded, confused, and demotivated by large doses of the unknown.

While personal strength and stamina may vary somewhat from individual to individual, most of us have a limited amount that we can bring to bear in a work situation. While we all may be able to work for short periods of time in a sprint mode, none of us can sprint a whole marathon. We can get in better shape and eat more nutritious food for added energy, but even that cannot add 10 or 20 hours to our productive work week for the long haul.

So, what's the point? In many of our organizations, we are attempting to run (or change) our employees beyond the limits imposed by Mother Nature. While most people can handle six to seven things on their plates, managers pile on 30! While most of us really need order and priority to make sense out of our world, managers label each of the 30 things "Top Priority." While many of us cannot handle high doses of uncertainty without shutdown, we hear managers say, "Things are changing so fast, we won't really be able to develop a firm vision or direction for some time to come. We'll just have to play it by ear." And, while most of us can handle a 50-hour week, we can't handle 60 to 70 hours week in and week out. That's especially true if the work is the 30-priority-one-items variety. We see organizations pushing employees beyond the limits, seemingly without realizing that there are limits.

Leaders must recognize the capacity of their employees and manage change realistically. It's the leader's job to tackle the analysis of the dozens of things her company might do, and then pick some. In fact, it's the leader's job to pick the short list she wants her company to focus on for the next time period. That will be the change agenda for the immediate future. It's our job as leaders to sort out the order and priority on the list of things to do.

And leaders must create some certainty out of even the most ambiguous situations. We've got to say, "I'm not sure what the future holds, and I've got no crystal ball; but for now, we're going north. When we get a little farther down the road, we will take another look. We might change our course, but for now we are northbound."

What if the leader is wrong? What if she picks the wrong change agenda or short list? She must still take the risk, drive the stake in the ground, and take a stand. It's her job as a leader to take the risk. Because of her position, she's in the best place to assess options and to manage risk. It's not her job to collect as many change items as she can find and rain them down on her troops. If she does that, she is not leading. She is overloading her organization and forcing her troops to use their own rationing schemes to decide what they will and will not do.

Limits Posed by the
Organization's Identity

MIND-CLEARING EXAMPLE

Imagine the director of a theater company who works for years to develop his company into a first-rate musical comedy team. Imagine the investors for the company sensing an opportunity in Shakespearean drama and insisting that the company do *Hamlet* as its next production. Also imagine that the investment offer carries a timetable for transitioning to *Hamlet* that is the same length as the one the company has been using to transition between musical comedies.

Just as individuals develop a persona over time, organizations develop an identity. By identity, we mean something akin to an organization's personality. As with an individual personality, we know that identity is associated with certain ways of being or behaving that are probably enduring and relatively stable. An organization develops its identity over time just as an individual develops her personality, over time and through many complex life experiences.

Organizational identity can be formed as the organization experiences success at doing one kind of thing and failure when doing another. Identity can be formed as an organization hires several individuals that have similar backgrounds, professions, or even personalities to do a certain kind of work. For example, we would think that sales organizations have more of an outgoing identity than an engineering organization, because managers tend to hire outgoing people as salesmen and analytical people as engineers.

Organizational identity is obviously not a limiting factor with the vast majority of organizational changes. The business changes initiated by most organizations are not so sweeping that they require totally different personnel, know-how, or approaches to work. There can be problems on a unit-by-unit basis within an organization, even in relatively minor organizational changes, if that unit is expected to perform beyond its identity. For example, we once worked around an organizational change that required a number of outside salesmen to relinquish most of their roles to another organization while they moved to more research and analytical duties behind the scenes. Using the terms of this discussion, the identity of this sales unit turned out to be too far from the requirements of the marketing job. Final resolution came only after the group of salesmen was dispersed to other sales units and several new hires were brought into the new marketing area.

The bottom line is again simple. The change leader must be sensitive to identity issues when deciding what organizational changes to make and how to make them. She must keep the constraint of identity in mind in both design and execution of change. Organizations that have mastered change have the ability to pull off some amazing transformations within their organization. But even masters of change must manage the kind and amount of change in recognition of both identity and human constraints.

MANAGING THE RATE OF ORGANIZATIONAL CHANGE

The change leader can manage change realistically by properly timing the organizational change, taking change capacity into account, and continually resourcing change.

Timing Organizational Change

 MIND-CLEARING EXAMPLE

Imagine the director of a theater company watching ticket sales decline steadily and waiting until the house is almost empty every night of the week before he decides that a new play is in order. Them imagine the director selecting and attempting to transition to a new play over a weekend.

The goal for timing an organizational change is simple to state but frequently very difficult to reach. The idea is to identify when the organization needs to have its change completed so that organizational goals in the marketplace can continue to be met. The theater director wants to transition to a new play before the old play goes into the tank and just as the hype for the new play reaches its peak. And the chief executive of the organization wants his change to work the same way.

Some of the primary factors that determine when an organization should change and how fast it should change are:

- The state and trends in the organization's current performance.
- The presence of business opportunities for those who can take advantage.
- How fast and how long those opportunities stay open.
- How fast the competitors are moving toward those opportunities.
- How soon the organization needs the projected business results of the change.

The goal is to be able to start an organizational change early enough so that the desired outcome of the change can be realized as needed, but not to start the change so early that it is difficult to make a convincing case for the change. We would like to think that the chief executive would initiate the organizational change based on a thorough and comprehensive analysis of the business situation. But in reality, the change decision is frequently made more at the gut level. And, of course, wouldn't life be wonderful for all of us if executives were able to anticipate the changes that need to be made and then be able to execute them in time to be able to keep organizational performance at a maximum.

The chief executive must pick and publicly commit to the target changeover date. The bottom line on timing organizational change is to pick a time. We have seem so many top managers sense the need for an organizational change, have an idea about when they would like to see the organization operating differently, but then never actually pick a time for the change. Most people in organizations are accustomed to responding to hard targets and hard dates. A top manager's failure to pick the target time for changeover ensures that the change effort will get off on the wrong foot. Failure to commit to a target time strongly communicates the message that we don't have to manage change like we manage the regular, run-the-business work of the organization.

The organization needs to hear the chief executive say out loud, "We need to have our change done by this date or we will not be able to take advantage of our opportunity (solve our problem, continue our current level of prosperity, etc.)"

Taking Change Capacity into Account

MIND-CLEARING EXAMPLE

Imagine the director of a theater company who insists on transitioning to a new play in two weeks, when he knows that his company (and the competing companies) require four weeks just for rehearsal. Imagine that the new play requires at least a month of set construction, rigging, and testing, according to the stage manager, who is considered to be one of the best in the business.

Top management must take their organization's demonstrated capacity for change into account when planning the number, sequence, and steps for change. A chief executive may be highly excited and enthusiastic about a new change initiative, but every organization has a capacity to change that must be taken into account. By change capacity, we mean the organization's capability to make change happen on target, on time, and on budget. Change capacity is not the same as the organization's goals and expectations for change. Change capacity is defined by the organization's actual track record in managing change.

An organization's capacity to change is determined primarily by the skills, experience, and courage the organization members have in change management. A key requirement for those executives whose job it is to manage the amount and rate of change in an organization is to stay tuned in to their organization's change capacity.

Just as the manager of a public sports arena knows with certainty how long it takes to change configuration from basketball to hockey, top management must know its organization's changeover time. The chief executive in many organizations has an intuitive sense about changeover times based on his experience in organizations. But we argue to our clients that identifying and understanding their organizations' track records of change is better than intuition. How many of us have had a hunch about how long it would take for an organizational change that turned out to be far off the mark.

Identifying an organization's change capacity is not as easy as it sounds. There are, however, some means that can be used to estimate an organization's change capacity:

- *Examine the organization's history of at least two or three changes of the type being considered.* This examination can be done with a small team of participants who were central in change management in each initiative. The team will probably have good recollection (or good calendars) that will allow them to peg the kind of change, the start and stop dates of the change project, and the time when the organization was estimated to be up and running with new work.

- *Examine a competitor's history of change, if you can find a competitor that resembles your organization* (odds are that you can). The marketplace knows when an organization is making a change of any size, and information will be available from customers, the competitor's former employees, trade organizations, or even the company's public documents. Occasionally we see change information in press releases. We even have one client organization that is so good at change that they openly tout their time to change to the folks in their distribution channels as a competitive superiority. This company, by the way, will not tout the method it uses for the change because it feels its method is a competitive edge.

- *Estimate change capacity at this point in time.* At any one point in time, an organization has a number of gun battles going on: dealing with regulatory changes, the loss (or addition) of players on the top management team, a major industry downturn, a war with a hostile competitor, and so on. In addition, the organization will likely be involved in a number of planned changes. Assessing the total amount of change activity and general extra stuff that is going on will allow an estimate of the organization's will to tackle another change at this time.

Estimating an organization's change capacity at a given point of time is indeed a difficult task, but a necessary one if any new change is to be well launched.

The chief executive must pick and publicly commit to the start date for change. Having some idea of change capacity and knowing the top executive's target for changeover allows the selection of the date for launching the change initiative. It is quite common for an organization to hear from a top manager, "We just received a big order from customer X and we are very excited about it. We start work on the order next week, and it will ship at the end of September." Our goal in mastering change is to be able to make similar announcements about organizational change initiatives like, "We need to have a new face on our customer service. We will have that new face on by the end of February of next year, and we are launching our change work next week."

Success of organizational change is rooted in understanding when a change is needed and planning a change that the organization is realistically capable of executing. We do not want mindless change (i.e., change for no good reason), and we do not want change that is launched with a mindless plan. Planning a change using knee jerk responses that don't match the organization's change capacity is a sure formula for launching a change that will be off target, off time and off budget. It is important to keep in mind that the primary driver of successful organizational change is not excitement and enthusiasm but realistic plans followed by step-by-step success.

Resourcing for the Needed Rate of Change

MIND-CLEARING EXAMPLE

Imagine the director of a theater company who puts her company on an unusually aggressive time schedule for the transition to a new play. Imagine that she is unwilling to schedule the theater for rehearsals on the needed days, not to mention being unwilling to pay the stage and lighting technicians overtime for the work they need to do to accommodate the aggressive schedule.

Top management must constantly provide the organization with the resources needed to complete targeted organizational change. Organizational change takes huge amounts of time and energy, and there is no escaping that fact. The time and energy required by change will be consumed while the organization is running its daily business of making products and serving clients. What we hope to escape is the excessive loss of time and resources that is almost always the result of poor change management. Therefore, top management must stay tuned in to the organization's change picture and work day to day to provide needed resources.

One of the most important jobs of the chief executive who must manage the portfolio of changes that may be going on in her organization is to keep her hand on the throttle of change by allocating (or denying) the resources needed for change. Given the certainty that the business environment will be changing and that there will be opportunities for the company to change its priorities for use of its funds, the chief executive is in a unique position to manage the overall change effort without getting into the details of any one change project. The chief executive's job is to allocate the needed organizational resources up front for the organization's program of change and then to keep those resources coming despite competing needs and priorities. The chief executive can access needed resources along the way by

- canceling some projects to free up resources,
- moving deadlines and time schedules,
- transferring funds and people between change projects (as well as between run-the-business and change-the-business initiatives), or
- hiring extra bodies (vendors/consultants) as needed to supplement internal resources.

We recommend the following do and don't guidelines to our clients who are managing multiple change efforts at the organizational level:

- Don't start if you can't resource the change or make up the resources along the way.
- Do get the change initiatives into the organization's budget to match the dollar results of the change with the costs of doing the change.
- Do manage the rate of change(s) to ensure that you make the overall desired progress as a company (remember, your goal is to have the company performing at the optimal level, not each individual unit in the company).
- Don't shy away from canceling parts of the change if that is what it takes to get overall results.
- Do remember that cancellation of a change initiative can be an act of courage and creativity.
- Top management must keep the throttles open for both running and changing the business—keeping in mind the organization's capacity. An organization can only do so much before it runs out of time and energy to do anything well. The manager's job is to keep an accurate, real-time assessment of the organization's change capacity—keeping in mind the limitations of the human beings involved as well as the identity of the organization.

PART SIX

Mastering Change

To be at peace with change, we must move organizations and individuals to a point where change responsibility and change expertise are as second nature as running their business. We cannot continue thinking about change as an ad hoc process that we can muddle through. Organizations and individuals must master change or they will be continuously out of sync in today's world of work.

11

The Organization and Employees Master Change

MIND-CLEARING EXAMPLE

Imagine a newly-formed theater company that goes into a panic when its first play begins to show a few empty seats. Imagine the director, the cast, and the crew wringing their hands and saying: "Wow, we weren't expecting this. I thought the plan was to just do *Hamlet* forever. We were planning to make our careers here. This was supposed to be a classic play that would always stay in demand. What are we to do?"

We know that a theater company goes into business with the idea of performing a long series of successful plays. The idea that no play will last forever is accepted by all associated with the company: its leaders, cast, and crew. Organizations and individuals will not have mastered change until they too understand that their organization's life must be made up of a series of performances that their changing customers will value over the long term. Individuals in organizations will not have mastered change until they can relish both today's performance and the opportunity to change periodically to a new and fresh play. As we will see in this chapter, change mastery must occur at both the organizational and individual worker levels.

MASTERING CHANGE AT THE ORGANIZATIONAL LEVEL

MIND-CLEARING EXAMPLE

Imagine the theater company that had no skills in moving from one production to another. Each time a play closes, the director starts all over again in thinking about what must be done to transition to a new play. Imagine there being no institutional memory in the theater company of how it made its last transition—what it did first, how it did it, who was best in transition work, etc.

Organizations must learn change and then build and institutionalize the organizational machinery needed to make successful change happen just as a theater company does. Organizations cannot afford to attack each new change as though it were a once-in-a-decade event.

Organizational Change Mastery: An Operational Definition

Defining change mastery for an organization may seem like a complex and theoretical exercise. But let's use our theater metaphor one more time and do some common sense translation to a business organization. We will say that, by definition, a successful theater company has mastered change. What change competencies do we expect that theatre company to have? We expect the company to be competent in

- identifying the time when its current successful play might need to change,
- identifying a new play that can follow its current play and add to the company's string of successes,
- resourcing the production of the new play (i.e., finding the dollars needed to bankroll the new play),
- signing up the cast and crew for performance of the new play,
- signing up the cast and crew to begin preparation for the new play before the current one ends,

- opening the new play with it more than 95 percent ready for Broadway,
- shutting down the old play to focus all resources on the new one, and
- refining the new play until it reaches and stays at least 99 percent ready for Broadway.

We believe that business organizations have mastered change when they can successfully and consistently perform on each of the eight dimensions of competence listed below.

1. *Identifying the time for change.* An organization that has mastered change will stay tuned to the business environment and its own internal business situation and will consistently identify the right time to begin a change as well as the target time for the completion of change.
2. *Identifying the vision for organizational change.* An organization that has mastered change will develop a vision that will be a detailed, valid business model that can be achieved with a high degree of confidence because of the organization's track record of change.
3. *Planning and resourcing the vision.* An organization that has mastered change will ensure that the financial, time, and human resources needed for the change will be made available for change success. The organization will determine its needed level of investment in change based on the value of the change to the organization as well as on the organization's track record of change costs. The organization will develop a change plan that will meet organizational needs while accommodating work needs of managers and employees.
4. *Enlisting the organization to go for the vision.* An organization that has mastered change will sign up all managers and the majority of workers for the vision, using the case for change as the basis for motivation and the needed sense of urgency. The organization will describe the impending change as needed and required to meet the organization's success targets.
5. *Enlisting the organization for completing change work and continuing existing work.* An organization that has mastered change will sign up all managers and workers to get the needed transition work done on target, on time, and on budget. The organization will make arrangements as needed to ensure that change

work and existing work can both be accomplished without compromising the motivation of the work force.

6. *Changing over to the vision with high performance and competence.* An organization that has mastered change will change over to the new way of operating called for by the vision for organizational change with most of the performance bugs all worked through.

7. *Stopping old work.* An organization that has mastered change will stop doing work the old way and shut down those parts of the operation that are no longer in sync with the vision. The organization will not wait until evidence of old operations forces it to complete the shutdown of the old way of doing business.

8. *Refining new work to the needed level.* An organization that has mastered change will rapidly work to refine its changed operations to reach the targeted and needed level of performance. The organization will not wait for customer or investor feedback to stimulate and motivate it to refine the play to the 99 percent of target level.

Theater companies must master change because it is the nature of their business. Doesn't it also make sense for today's business organizations to strive for change mastery since it is the nature of business today?

Developing the Organization toward Change Mastery

How does an organization move toward change mastery? The quick answer is very slowly with a lot of trials and errors. The better answer might be to follow the five-step change model that has been at the heart of this book.

Step 1: Develop a vision of change mastery for the organization. Although many organizations identify innovation or creativity as parts of their vision or strategy for the future, few organizations describe the details of what those words mean. If an organization is betting on innovation, creativity, or agility for part of its future success, the organization would do well to describe what it means in terms of change mastery. We recommend that our clients decide how they want to handle change and to come up with some words or ideas about what they expect.

What does a vision of change mastery look like and how do you develop one? A relatively easy way to develop a vision of change mastery is to use or modify the operational definition of change mastery and its eight dimensions that we covered in the previous section. Put your version of that change definition in front of your managers and they will begin to understand what is expected from them as the organization's primary change team.

Step 2: Develop or alter work processes to enable change mastery. Although many organizations have work processes for assessing the business environment and periodic strategic planning, most do not yet have formalized work processes that are desperately needed for change mastery. We feel that the following three work processes or disciplines are critical for organizations to develop on their way to change mastery:

1. *A program management process.* This allows the organization to effectively manage multiyear change initiatives of strategic value (like cost reduction or customer relations optimization). Program management provides the facility to identify and manage multiple organizational changes (including multiple change projects) simultaneously while the organization is continuing to run-the-business.

   The program management processes that we see today are usually owned by an organization that reports to the senior executive of the company. This program management unit serves as the change-the-business structure (or office) that helps manage the continuous conflict and balance that is needed between the run-the-business and change-the-business agendas.

   Failure to adopt a program management process or to set up a program office will ensure that the organization will not do a good job managing change in the face of day-to-day business. The program office gives the chief executive the support she needs as she does her job as the chief change officer, whose job it is to move the organization toward a series of successful futures while meeting yearly run-the-business targets.

2. *A project management process.* This gives the capability to bring concrete results to a given change initiative in a defined time period. The organization must have a required project management method that provides detailed guidance on how to manage every change project (using steps from the change management method as the key activities to be managed).

The project management processes that we see in organizations today are usually owned by one of the technical departments like engineering or information technology. For change mastery, the program management office must identify the version of the organization's project management method that will be best suited for change projects and require that the project management method be used on all changes of significant size.

Failure to adopt a project management method will ensure that the organization will not do a good job managing change, and that the change initiatives that the organization attempts to run simultaneously will not be comparable, making overall program management practically impossible to do well.

3. *A change management process.* This gives detailed steps on how to make organizational change happen in a controlled and predictable way. The organization must have a required change management method (like the one described in this book) that gives detailed guidance on how to employ the means of change (i.e., process alterations, employee performance changes, etc.) to alter the means of doing business (i.e., how the company delivers its products and services to customers, etc.).

The change management processes that we see in organizations today are usually ad hoc and informal or "processes de jour," depending on which change management consultants just made a sale to the chief executive. Progressive organizations that have mastered change place the ownership for the organization's change management method in the hands of the program office (or their organization's equivalent).

Failure to adopt a change management method will ensure that the organization will not be successful in change projects, despite the level of effectiveness of program and project management. The organization's change management method provides the content of activities and tasks needed for effective project management.

Step 3: Alter organizational tools to enable change mastery.

- *Management tools.* While most organizations have more than enough tools for the fundamental level of change competence, many of these tools need to be tuned to meet the needs of change mastery. Critical tools are critical path planning and multiproject management tools. Odds are that most organizations are already using these kinds of tools in the everyday work of running the business. Generic versions of these tools that can be used for change management are needed.

- *Reporting tools.* Most organizations have reporting tools that allow management to understand results and progress of the organization toward its run-the-business agenda. These reporting tools will need to be altered somewhat to allow management to see the progress in the change agenda (i.e., the change program/projects) alongside regular business goals.

Step 4: Modify the performance management system to enable change mastery.

- *Employee roles.* Organizations that have mastered change have set clear expectation for managers and employees alike — that change is a part of doing business and all workers are expected to be willing and responsible for change. Roles for all workers must be modified to make such change expectations clear and a part of the workers' agreement with the company.

- *Employee training.* More managers today are receiving training in change management. This training must be extended beyond the usual "how human beings deal with change" to "what management must do to enable an organization to successfully change." We believe that it is critical for managers to know the actions they are responsible for taking to ensure that the mechanical attributes of their organizations are aligned with designated changes.

- *Employee performance evaluation.* Organizations that have mastered change realize that change performance counts. That is, these companies give employees informal feedback and formal performance evaluations on how well they are doing at change. Failure to give employees feedback/evaluation on change performance signals to employees that change doesn't count.

- *Employee compensation.* We believe it is critical to pay for what the organization needs, and not to pay for what the organization doesn't need. If we want the organization and its employees to master change, we must compensate those employees who contribute to both run the business and change the business. Employees who only contribute to the running of the business must have their compensation suffer and their jobs put at risk.

Step 5: Plan, schedule, and manage the way to change mastery. An organization's journey toward change mastery must be treated like any other organizational change. Failure to consider change mastery as a project will delay the organization's journey although the trip might not be totally stopped. As the organization makes progress on other change initiatives over time, some change mastery progress will still be made.

Assessment of an Organization's Level of Change Mastery

Organizations can gain value in their efforts to improve change mastery by having senior managers individually assess what the organization does well and not so well, followed by a management team discussion of those assessments and the reasons for them. We believe that the best way to examine an organization's level of change mastery is to look at what we call results-based criteria and means-based criteria. The two lists of criteria below have proven to be very useful stimulators of conversation among managers interested in improving their organization's level of change mastery.

Results-Based Assessment of Level of Organizational Change Mastery

1. Identifying the Time for Change

   Our organization consistently picks what turn out to be good times to change.

   (Consistently untrue) 1 2 3 4 5 6 7 (Consistently true)

2. Identifying the Vision for Organizational Change

   Our organization consistently develops a clear and valid picture of the future we need to create.

   (Consistently untrue) 1 2 3 4 5 6 7 (Consistently true)

3. Resourcing the Vision

   Our organization does not launch a change until adequate resources have been arranged.

   (Consistently untrue) 1 2 3 4 5 6 7 (Consistently true)

4. Enlisting the Organization to Go for the Vision

   Our organization is consistently successful in getting the organization members to sign up for the change.

   (Consistently untrue) 1 2 3 4 5 6 7 (Consistently true)

5. Enlisting the Organization for Change Work and Continuing Old Work

   Our organization is consistently successful in completing change work on time without a significant loss in productivity in the old work we were doing before the change.

   (Consistently untrue) 1 2 3 4 5 6 7 (Consistently true)

6. Change Over to the Vision with 95 Percent Performance and Confidence

   Our organization is consistently successful changing over to new work that is performed from the start at 95 percent of target level.

   (Consistently untrue) 1 2 3 4 5 6 7 (Consistently true)

7. Stopping Old Work

   Our organization is consistently successful at shutting down old ways of doing business at the same time that we start the new way of doing business.

   (Consistently untrue) 1 2 3 4 5 6 7 (Consistently true)

8. Refining New Work to the Needed Level

   Our organization is consistently successful at refining our new way of operating to the 99 percent level within a short period of time.

   (Consistently untrue) 1 2 3 4 5 6 7 (Consistently true)

Means-Based Assessment of Level
of Change Mastery

1. Program Management

   Our chief executive acts as the owner of our program of change (our change agenda).

   (Consistently untrue) 1 2 3 4 5 6 7 (Consistently true)

   Our organization has a formal capability for the identification, planning, launch, and management of sets of initiatives designed to move our organization toward a series of successful futures.

   (Consistently untrue) 1 2 3 4 5 6 7 (Consistently true)

   Our organization formally manages our change program right alongside our normal run-the-business operations.

   (Consistently untrue) 1 2 3 4 5 6 7 (Consistently true)

2. Project Management

   Our organization has a formal, required method and capability for the management of individual change projects.

   (Consistently untrue) 1 2 3 4 5 6 7 (Consistently true)

   Every change project has an appointed project manager who ensures that the project management method is flexible, but consistently applied.

   (Consistently untrue) 1 2 3 4 5 6 7 (Consistently true)

   Every project manager reports both to a line manager in the organization undergoing the change and to the program manager whose responsibility is to coordinate all change projects.

   (Consistently untrue) 1 2 3 4 5 6 7 (Consistently true)

3. Change Management

   Our organization has a formal, required method and capability for the management of organizational changes.

   (Consistently untrue) 1 2 3 4 5 6 7 (Consistently true)

Our managers are trained in change management and are willing and able to successfully direct their organizational units toward designated organizational changes.

(Consistently untrue) 1 2 3 4 5 6 7 (Consistently true)

Our workers understand the need to periodically change the play and are willing and able participants in organizational change.

(Consistently untrue) 1 2 3 4 5 6 7 (Consistently true)

MASTERING CHANGE AT THE INDIVIDUAL LEVEL

 MIND-CLEARING EXAMPLE

Imagine a theater company that is stunned to hear that its play will close. Imagine the performers feeling betrayed; insisting that life as they know it is over for them; crying out in anguish at the thought of having to learn new lines in a new play and having to give up their old costumes or their special places to stand on the stage.

While today's employees have been forced to deal with change, most have not as yet fully accepted the reality of continued change and the requirement to take full responsibility for making that change productive for both the organization and themselves. Today's employees have not yet accepted the mindset of professional actors who are fully responsible for their own performance in what will inevitably be a series of plays. In short, today's employees must learn change just like their brothers and sisters in the theater, or they should not expect successful work careers.

Individual Change Mastery:
An Operational Definition

Defining change mastery for an individual in a work organization is easily done with the use of our theater metaphor. We will say that, by definition, a successful, professional actor has mastered change by:

- Staying alert and attuned to the ongoing success of the current production in which he plays
- Understanding the time when the theater company might need to transition to a new performance
- Providing input to the theater company or director in discussions about possible new productions
- Pursuing, negotiating, and contracting for a role in the new production
- Following the lead of the director and working cooperatively with the remainder of the cast in rehearsing and developing his role in the new play
- Ensuring that he has fully developed his role and integrated it into the overall production in time for opening night
- Cooperatively working with the company to close out the old production
- Giving his best performance in the new play and taking the initiative to refine his role under the leadership of the director

We believe that individual workers in organizations have mastered change when they can successfully and consistently perform on each of the eight dimensions of competence listed below:

1. *Staying alert and attuned to organizational success.* An individual employee who has mastered change will stay tuned to the business environment and her organization's level of success — with customers, with investors, and with employees.
2. *Understanding the time for organizational change.* An individual employee who has mastered change will understand and appreciate the need to make changes in the organization and the subsequent need for alteration of her role. The employee will be able to look ahead to a series of roles over time as the organization continues to change to stay successful.
3. *Providing input about the future.* An individual employee who has mastered change will provide information to her manager

and others about what the organization might do and how it might do it for future success.

4. *Actively contracting for a role in the new work of the organization.* An individual employee who has mastered change will be alert to new roles she can play after the change or to changes in her current role. The individual employee will proactively come to the table to discuss, negotiate, and sign up for a role in the change.

5. *Taking the initiative to develop the new work role.* An individual employee who has mastered change will responsibly develop her new or altered role with the leadership of her manager and in cooperation with fellow workers in her organizational unit.

6. *Changing over to the new work role with high performance.* An individual employee who has mastered change will changeover on schedule to the new way of operating called for by the vision for organizational change. By changeover, the individual employee will have worked through the vast majority of the details in the new role and will be able to perform that role with high competence and confidence.

7. *Stopping old work.* An individual employee who has mastered change will stop doing work the old way and shut down those parts of her role that are no longer in sync with the vision. The individual employee will not wait for feedback from the manager to discontinue performance in the old role.

8. *Refining the new work role to the needed performance level.* An individual employee who has mastered change will rapidly work to refine her changed role to reach the targeted and needed level of performance. The individual employee will not wait for customer or manager feedback to stimulate and motivate her to refine her performance to the 99 percent level.

Professional actors in theater companies must master change because it is the nature of their business. Doesn't it also make sense for today's individual workers in other kinds of organizations to strive for change mastery because change seems to be the nature of business today?

Individual Development
toward Change Mastery:
The Right Perspective

The good news is that individuals have already mastered change. The bad news is that our change mastery is usually limited to our personal lives, not our business lives. In the first chapter of this book I talked about the fact that human beings have already mastered the ability to change in their personal lives long before they reach work organizations. The challenge for individual change mastery at work, therefore, is one of attitude, mindset, and perspective, not adding capabilities. Over the years we have developed and tested a mindset that seems to work rather easily for individuals as they attempt to resolve workplace change issues and challenges. We urge employees to develop a perspective that we call the *two-track mind.*

Today's employee must have a two-track mind to successfully navigate a rapidly changing business environment. Just as the term *one-track mind* connotes a passion and focus to get results, the employee must have that same passion and focus in two separate but interacting result areas. On track 1, the employee takes responsibility and acts for personal business success (like a successful career as an actor). On track 2, the employee takes responsibility and acts for the success of the organization or enterprise that employees him (focusing on one play at a time and doing his best to make that the best play ever).

Track 1 leads toward the personal success of the employee. The employee is now, and always has been, a one-person small business, a one-man band out to get personal results. It's really not a tough concept. Even Uncle Sam gets it. When each of us signs that IRS Form 1040 on April 15, we sign as a one-person economic unit — a money-making, revenue-earning, self-enterprise.

Being on track 1 means focusing on long-term personal viability and profitability of our one-person enterprise, (i.e. one's acting career). And like any enterprise, to achieve economic success the individual must sell something that others value. The something sold is service to someone or some economic enterprise, and the price for that service varies with the service's contribution to the success of the employing enterprise.

Like any enterprise, the individual must constantly publicize, market, and sell his services. The services that he sells change over time as the buyer, the employing organization, expresses the need for different things. An individual focusing on track 1 does internal research and development on his own nickel to ensure that he will have an acceptable service to sell. The person who has mastered change takes the initiative to develop the knowledge and skills necessary to continue to sell his services to the current employing organization — and the next ones.

An employee on track 1 has his act together as a one-person business, is in control of his own destiny, is responsible for his own development, and is earning his own economic results. An employee off track 1 does not take responsibility for his own situation in business life. The off-track employee depends on someone (a manager, a team, or a company) to steer him toward the right work, the right training, and the right career. Employees off track 1 are headed for personal economic disaster as they trust in some unseen hand to keep them sailing smoothly in tough competitive times.

Track 2 leads toward the success of the organization that employs the individual. The name of the game for this employing organization is long-term survival and profitability. Each organization must develop its own formula for success (i.e., find a winning play) in the competitive marketplace and then work day by day and year by year to put that formula into action (producing a series of winning plays). On track 2, the employee accepts the responsibility for the success of the employing organization. Today's employee recognizes that his personal success can be assured only by his contribution to the success of his employer.

An employee on track 2 is constantly attuned to the formula for the success of his employer. He identifies the personal contribution that he can make to organizational success and takes the initiative to make success happen. An on-track employee does not wait to be empowered. He assumes from the moment of employment that he has been given the go-ahead to contribute to the profitable business of the organization. An employee on track 2 takes the initiative to alter his services to the employing company as the company calls for organizational change, just as an actor takes the responsibility to develop her new role in the theater company's new play.

An employee off track 2 tries to contribute but doesn't want to follow the company's formula for success or its plan for organizational change, like an actor who wants to argue with the new script for the play or the director's plans for transitioning to that new play. An off-track employee wants to focus on the mechanics of the job that he has accepted without taking the responsibility to think beyond the job for company success. And the really off-track employee manages to mix both tracks. This employee cries, "If only my employer would change the way the company does business, then I would feel better about my personal success," like the actor who attributes his bad feelings solely to the quality of the script that has been written for the new play.

Today's employee will be successful at mastering change — if and only if — he or she is on track 1 and on track 2. Failure to use the two-track mind mires the employee in bad feelings about both self and employer and ensures there will be no change mastery. There are no compromises or short cuts. The employee must simultaneously focus on and balance both tracks because personal success and contribution-to-employer success go hand in hand.

Assessment of an Individual Employee's Level of Change Mastery

For a full understanding of an organization's level of change mastery, we must have some idea of how individuals in the organization handle change. A discussion of the following criteria should provide some very valuable ideas and directions for supporting change development for individual employees.

1. Staying Alert and Attuned to Organizational Success

   Our individual employees consistently seek information about the state of the company and how well it is meeting the expectations of customers, investors, and employees.

   (Consistently untrue) 1 2 3 4 5 6 7 (Consistently true)

2. Understanding the Time for Organizational Change

   Our individual employees consistently grasp and appreciate the need to make changes in the organization in order to stay competitive in our business and industry.

   (Consistently untrue) 1 2 3 4 5 6 7 (Consistently true)

3. Providing Input about the Future

   Our individual employees consistently offer ideas to management about the kinds of organizational changes the company might need to make for continuing success as well as suggestions about how those changes might be made.

   (Consistently untrue) 1 2 3 4 5 6 7 (Consistently true)

4. Actively Contracting for a Role after Organizational Change

   Our individual employees consistently discuss, negotiate, and sign up for their new roles that will take effect after the upcoming organizational change.

   (Consistently untrue) 1 2 3 4 5 6 7 (Consistently true)

5. Taking the Initiative to Develop the New Work Role

   Our individual employees consistently work aggressively to think through and prepare for the new work roles they will play after changeover.

   (Consistently untrue) 1 2 3 4 5 6 7 (Consistently true)

6. Changing Over to the New Work Role with High Performance and Competence

   Our individual employees consistently prepare for their new or altered roles so that they are able to give a 95 percent performance immediately after changeover.

   (Consistently untrue) 1 2 3 4 5 6 7 (Consistently true)

7. Stopping Old Work

   Our individual employees consistently stop the parts of their job that are no longer a part of their new or altered roles.

   (Consistently untrue) 1 2 3 4 5 6 7 (Consistently true)

8. Refining the New Work Role to the Needed Performance Level

   Our individual employees consistently refine their new or altered roles to the needed performance level.

   (Consistently untrue) 1 2 3 4 5 6 7 (Consistently true)

CHANGE IS THE RULE: CONCLUSION

This book actually has a pretty simple and straightforward message. As we have moved to a time in history when change in organizations is the rule and not the exception, we have come face to face with the requirement to master change. No longer can we muddle through changes in organizations as managers or workers. We must all face up to the need to become really proficient at managing change and become as good at it as we are at running the business.

We can learn so much about mastering change through the simple metaphor of the theater company, where change is the nature of the business. Our challenge in business organizations is to become as good at changing our organization as an experienced theater company is at changing performances. Our challenge as individuals in business organizations is to become as excited and proficient at change as are professional actors who understand that no play runs forever and that change provides career-building opportunities.

Now is the time to put down this book and step back into the daily world of organizational change. My wish for you is a positive and exciting future. "It's show time. Break a leg."

Recommended Resources

The Challenge of Change in Organizations: Helping Employees Thrive in the New Frontier. Nancy J. Barger and Linda K. Kirby (Davies-Black Publishing, 1995).

Champions of Change: How CEOs and Their Companies Are Mastering the Skills of Radical Change. David A. Nadler with Mark B. Nadler (Jossey-Bass Publishers, 1998).

Change at Work. Peter Cappelli, Laurie Bassi, Harry Katz, David Knoke, Paul Osterman, and Michael Useem (Oxford University Press, 1997).

Change at Work: A Comprehensive Management Process for Transforming Organizations. Oscar G. Mink, Pieter Ester Huysen, and Barbara Mink (Jossey-Bass Publishers, 1993).

The Change Management Toolkit: A Step-by-Step Methodology for Successfully Implementing Dramatic Organizational Change. Gary Skarke, Dutch Holland, Bill Rogers, and Diane Landon (WinHope Press, 1999).

Communicating Change: How to Win Employee Support for New Business Directions. Sandar Larkin (Contributor) and TJ Larkin (McGraw-Hill, Inc., 1994).

Discontinuous Change: Leading Organizational Transformation. David A. Nadler, et al, (Jossey-Bass Publishers, 1995).

Driving Change: How the Best Companies Are Preparing for the 21st Century. Jerry Yoram Wind and Jeremy Main (Free Press, 1998).

The Human Side of Change: A Practical Guide to Organizational Redesign. Timothy J. Galpin (Jossey-Bass Publishers, 1996).

Innovation and Entrepreneurship: Practice and Principles. Peter F. Drucker (Harperbusiness, 1993).

Leading Change. John P. Kotter (Harvard Business School Press, 1996).

Leading Change: Overcoming the Ideology of Comfort and the Tyranny of Custom. James O'Toole (Jossey-Bass Publishers, 1995).

Managing at the Speed of Change: How Resilient Managers Succeed and Prosper Where Others Fail. Daryl R. Conner (Villard Books, 1993).

Navigating Change: How CEOs, Top Teams, and Boards Steer Transformation. Edited by Donald C. Hambrick, David A. Nadler, and Michael L. Tushman (Harvard Business School Press, 1997).

Taking Charge of Change: 10 Principles for Managing People and Performance. Douglas K. Smith (Perseus Press, 1997).

Index